THE
creative
CHRISTMAS
KITCHEN

*A*s a place of sweet aromas and gentle nurturing, the kitchen is the heart of the home. With such a heritage, this cozy room quite naturally becomes the center of our holiday preparations. Tasteful gifts, festive parties, and even homemade ornaments are created there with loving hands and giving hearts.

The Creative Christmas Kitchen *is filled with new, exciting projects and ideas for the holidays, all prepared in the kitchen or created with foods and other items found there. You'll discover wonderful gifts and delicious dishes, along with decorations to bring holiday spirit into the kitchen — or any room of the house. May this book bring an added measure of love and joy to your Christmas celebration.*

Anne Childs

LEISURE ARTS, INC.
Little Rock, Arkansas

THE *creative* CHRISTMAS KITCHEN

EDITORIAL STAFF

Editor: Anne Van Wagner Childs
Executive Director: Sandra Graham Case
Creative Art Director: Gloria Bearden
Executive Editor: Susan Frantz Wiles

PRODUCTION
TECHNICAL
Managing Editor: Sherry Taylor O'Connor
Senior Technical Writer: Kathy Rose Bradley
Technical Writers: Dawn R. Kelliher, Nancy L. Taylor, and Candice Treat Murphy

DESIGN
Design Director: Patricia Wallenfang Sowers
Designers: Diana Heien Suttle, Mary Lillian Hill, and Rebecca Werle

FOODS
Foods Editor: Susan Warren Reeves, R.D.
Assistant Foods Editor: Jane Kenner Prather
Test Kitchen Assistant: Nora Faye Spencer Clift

EDITORIAL
Associate Editor: Dorothy Latimer Johnson
Senior Editorial Writer: Linda L. Trimble
Editorial Writers: Laurie R. Burleson, Robyn Sheffield-Edwards, and Barbara Cameron Ford
Advertising and Direct Mail Copywriters: Steven M. Cooper and Marla Shivers

ART
Production Art Director: Melinda Stout
Senior Production Artist: Michael Spigner
Photography Stylists: Sondra Harrison Daniel, Karen Smart Hall, Judith Howington Merritt, and Charlisa Erwin Parker
Typesetters: Cindy Lumpkin and Stephanie Cordero
Advertising and Direct Mail Artist: Linda Lovette

BUSINESS STAFF

Publisher: Steve Patterson
Controller: Tom Siebenmorgen
Retail Sales Director: Richard Tignor
Retail Marketing Director: Pam Stebbins
Retail Customer Services Director: Margaret Sweetin
Marketing Manager: Russ Barnett

Executive Director of Marketing and Circulation: Guy A. Crossley
Fulfillment Manager: Byron L. Taylor
Print Production: Nancy Reddick Lister and Laura Lockhart

MEMORIES IN THE MAKING SERIES

International Standard Book Number 0-942237-18-8

Table of Contents

Table of Contents

Table of Contents

*C*hristmas is a time for giving, and gifts created in your kitchen are a special way to share a little of yourself. As we lovingly prepare each delicious offering, our hearts are filled with the joyous spirit of the season. This collection of holiday treats features scrumptious recipes that will surprise and charm your loved ones and friends. We've also included a variety of simple crafts and ideas for attractive packaging to enhance your presentations. Your warm wishes will come shining through in each and every gift.

TASTY GIFTS FOR THE SEASON

SPIRITED SAUCE

*F*or a spirited finale to a holiday meal, Brandied Strawberries can't be beat! The colorful mixture of berries, brown sugar, and brandy is delicious spooned over cake or ice cream. To present the sauce, tuck a jar in a decorated basket along with a ribbon-tied pound cake made from your favorite recipe.

BRANDIED STRAWBERRIES

1½ cups firmly packed brown
     sugar
1 cup water
1 package (16 ounces) frozen
    unsweetened strawberries,
    thawed and drained
¼ cup lemon juice
½ cup brandy

In a large saucepan, combine sugar and water. Stirring constantly, cook over medium heat until sugar dissolves. Stir in strawberries and lemon juice. Bring to a boil and cook 10 minutes. Remove from heat; stir in brandy. Store in an airtight container in refrigerator or follow Canning Instructions, page 124, processing in boiling water bath 15 minutes. Serve with cake or ice cream. Include serving suggestions with gift.

Yield: about 1½ pints

HEARTY HOLIDAY BREAKFAST

Christmas morning calls for a special breakfast treat, and Almond Pancake Mix is sure to fill the bill! A friend can easily make a batch of the nutty-tasting wheat cakes for a healthy, hearty beginning to the holiday celebration. Package the mix in a festive bag and team it with a griddle and spatula for a gourmet gift that's guaranteed to please.

ALMOND PANCAKE MIX

    3 cups nonfat dry milk
 2½ cups all-purpose flour
    1 cup whole-wheat flour
    1 cup finely ground almonds
    ⅔ cup baking powder
    ⅓ cup granulated sugar
    1 tablespoon salt

In a large bowl, stir all ingredients together until well blended. Store in a resealable plastic bag. Give with recipe for pancakes.

Yield: about 7½ cups pancake mix, enough for 3 batches of pancakes

To make pancakes: In a medium bowl, combine 2½ cups pancake mix, 1¼ cups water, 1 egg, and 2 tablespoons vegetable oil. Stir just until moistened. Heat a greased griddle over medium heat. For each pancake, pour about ¼ cup batter onto griddle and cook until top of pancake is full of bubbles and underside is golden brown.

Turn with a spatula and cook until remaining side is golden brown. Regrease griddle as necessary. Serve with butter and syrup.

Yield: about 1 dozen 5-inch pancakes

For fabric bag, use a 10½" x 40" fabric piece and follow Steps 2 and 4 of Fabric Bag instructions, page 122; press top edge of bag 5" to wrong side. For

label, follow manufacturer's instructions to apply paper-backed fusible web to wrong side of a 4" square of white fabric; cut a 2" x 3" piece from fused fabric. Use a permanent felt-tip pen to write ''ALMOND PANCAKE MIX'' on label and to draw a line around edge. Fuse label to bag. Place a plastic bag of mix in bag. Tie an 18" length of ½"w ribbon into a bow around top of bag.

SAUCY CRANBERRY CHUTNEY

Spiced with cinnamon and cloves, this tangy Cranberry Chutney is a delicious new way to serve cranberries. The lightly sweetened condiment adds saucy flavor to meats or cream cheese and crackers. For giving, a shiny foil bag makes a nice package, especially when decorated with a special ornament for the tree.

CRANBERRY CHUTNEY

- 1 tablespoon vegetable oil
- ¼ cup finely chopped celery
- 2 tablespoons finely chopped onion
- 1 can (16 ounces) whole berry cranberry sauce
- ¼ cup red wine vinegar
- 1 tablespoon honey
- ½ teaspoon ground cinnamon
- ¼ teaspoon ground cloves

In a small skillet, heat oil over medium heat. Add celery and onion; cook until tender. Spoon celery mixture into a medium bowl. Add remaining ingredients and stir until well blended. Pour into a container, cover, and refrigerate 8 hours or overnight to allow flavors to blend. Serve with meat, cream cheese and crackers, or bread. Include serving suggestions with gift.

Yield: about 2 cups chutney

YUMMY DOG TREATS

Even an old dog might learn a new trick for these wholesome hearts! Our simple recipe for Doggie Biscuits, flavored with beef and bacon, is a great way to keep the cupboard full of the yummy canine treats. A cleverly decorated container, complete with a bright new dog collar, makes this gift the "best of show."

DOGGIE BISCUITS

- 1 teaspoon instant beef bouillon
- ½ cup hot water
- 2¼ cups whole-wheat flour
- ½ cup nonfat dry milk
- ⅓ cup vegetable oil
- 1 jar (about 3¼ ounces) bacon-flavored pieces
- 1 tablespoon firmly packed brown sugar
- 1 egg

Preheat oven to 300 degrees. In a medium bowl, dissolve bouillon in water. Add remaining ingredients, stirring until well blended. On a lightly floured surface, use a floured rolling pin to roll out dough to ⅛-inch thickness. Use a 2-inch heart-shaped cookie cutter to cut out dough. Transfer to a greased baking sheet. Bake 30 to 35 minutes or until firm. Transfer to a wire rack to cool completely. Store in an airtight container.

Yield: about 6 dozen doggie biscuits

BISCUIT JAR

You will need a canister with flat lid, fabric, paper, permanent felt-tip pen with fine point, miniature holly garland, craft glue, matte clear acrylic spray, and a dog collar to fit neck of canister.

1. Cut a circle from fabric to fit on top of canister lid. Cut a circle from paper smaller than fabric circle. Use pen to write "FOR GOOD LITTLE DOGS" on paper circle.

2. Glue fabric circle, then paper circle, to lid. Glue holly garland along edge of fabric circle. Allow to dry.

3. Allowing to dry between coats, apply 2 coats of acrylic spray to lid.

4. Place collar around neck of canister.

CHRISTMAS CAKE

*D*electable cakes are always welcome holiday gifts, and this Sugar-and-Spice Pound Cake is sure to please. The moist cake is richly flavored with ginger, nutmeg, and plum jam. A candy-striped gift box decorated with a chain of gingerbread men makes a cute container for your gift.

SUGAR-AND-SPICE POUND CAKE

     1 cup butter or margarine, softened
  1½ cups granulated sugar
     5 eggs
     1 cup plum jam or preserves
     ½ cup whipping cream
  2½ cups all-purpose flour
     2 teaspoons ground ginger
     1 teaspoon baking powder
     ½ teaspoon ground nutmeg
     ½ teaspoon baking soda
     ¼ teaspoon salt

Preheat oven to 325 degrees. In a large bowl, cream butter and sugar until fluffy using an electric mixer. Add eggs, one at a time, beating well after each addition. Stir in jam and cream. In a medium bowl, sift together remaining ingredients. Add dry ingredients to creamed mixture; beat until smooth. Pour batter into a greased and floured 10-inch tube pan. Bake 1 hour to 1 hour 5 minutes, testing for doneness with a toothpick. Cool in pan 10 minutes. Remove from pan. Cool completely on a wire rack. Store in an airtight container.

Yield: about 20 servings

For 10″ cake box, follow Gift Box instructions, page 122. For gingerbread men, cut a 5″ x 40½″ strip of brown craft paper. Spacing folds 3⅜″ apart, fanfold paper strip. For pattern, follow Tracing Patterns, page 122. Center pattern on folded strip; draw around pattern. Cut out gingerbread man along solid lines only; unfold strip. Use black dimensional paint in squeeze bottle for eyes and white dimensional paint in squeeze bottle for detail lines; allow to dry. Use spray adhesive to glue strip around box. We decorated our box with 1⅞″w wired ribbon.

TEATIME DELIGHT

Aromatic and spicy, cup of tea made with our range-Nutmeg Tea Mix ill add holiday flavor to reakfast or teatime. To are with a friend, package e mix in a pretty box and ck it in a festive gift bag. purchased teapot-shaped rnament provides a hint f the treat that's inside.

ORANGE-NUTMEG TEA MIX

- 1 cup unsweetened powdered instant tea
- 1 cup granulated sugar
- 1 package (0.15 ounces) unsweetened orange-flavored soft drink mix
- 1 teaspoon ground nutmeg

In a small bowl, combine all gredients; stir until well blended. ore in an airtight container. Give with erving instructions.

ield: about 1⅔ cups tea mix

o serve: Stir 2 tablespoons tea mix into ounces hot or cold water.

r gift bag, trim top edge of a gift bag desired finished height; cut scallops ong top edge. Use a hole punch to unch evenly spaced holes approx. " apart 1″ from top edge of bag. eginning and ending at center front, read ⅝″w ribbon through holes. Tie bbon into a bow and trim ends. Hang esired ornament around bow. Line bag ith a fabric square.

15

"STAINED GLASS" BRITTLE

Crushed hard candies add bright colors and fruity flavors to "Stained Glass" brittle. A variation of the traditional brittle recipe, the candy is perfect for sharing at Christmas. A candle and holly design appliquéd in shiny lamé fabrics creates the look of a stained glass window atop the gift tin.

"STAINED GLASS" BRITTLE

¾ cup coarsely crushed assorted
 fruit-flavored, ring-shaped
 hard candies (about 7 rolls)
1½ cups granulated sugar
½ cup light corn syrup
¼ cup water
1½ tablespoons butter or margarine
½ teaspoon salt
1 teaspoon baking soda

Spread crushed candies evenly in a buttered 10 x 15-inch jellyroll pan. Butter sides of a 3-quart heavy saucepan or Dutch oven. Combine next 4 ingredients in pan. Stirring constantly, cook over medium-low heat until sugar dissolves. Using a pastry brush dipped in hot water, wash down any sugar crystals on sides of pan. Attach candy thermometer to pan, making sure thermometer does not touch bottom of pan. Increase heat to medium and bring to a boil. Do not stir while syrup is boiling. Continue to cook until syrup reaches hard crack stage (approximately 300 to 310 degrees) and turns light golden in color. Test about ½ teaspoon syrup in ice water. Syrup should form brittle threads in ice water and remain brittle when removed from water. Remove from heat and add butter and salt; stir until butter melts. Add soda (syrup will foam); stir until soda dissolves. Pour syrup over candies. Using a buttered spatula, spread syrup to edges of pan. Cool completely. Break into pieces. Store in an airtight container.

Yield: about 1¼ pounds brittle

"STAINED GLASS" TIN

You will need a tin with lid at least 7½" square, gold and white spray paint, an 8" square of gold lamé fabric, a 4" x 7" piece of green lamé fabric, a 6" square of red lamé fabric, a 4" x 7" piece of white fabric, tracing paper, lightweight fusible interfacing, paper-backed fusible web, removable fabric marking pen, black dimensional fabric paint in a squeeze bottle, a 6¼" square of medium weight cardboard, craft batting, craft glue, 1 yd of ¼" dia. metallic red twisted cord, hot glue gun, and glue sticks.

1. Paint tin gold and lid white; allow to dry. Set aside.
2. Follow manufacturers' instructions to apply interfacing, then web, to wrong sides of red, green, and white fabrics.
3. Trace berry, flame, and leaf cluster patterns onto tracing paper; cut out. Use patterns to cut pieces from indicated fabrics.
4. For candles, cut one 1¼" x 3" and two 1¼" x 2½" pieces from white fabric.
5. Round off corners of cardboard square. Center cardboard on right side of gold lamé; use fabric marking pen to draw around square. Remove cardboard.
6. Referring to photo, position candles, flames, leaf clusters, and berries in drawn square on gold lamé; fuse in place.
7. Referring to photo, use black paint to paint over raw edges of appliqués, to paint detail lines, and to paint over pen line. Following paint manufacturer's recommendations for drying time, allow to dry.
8. Cut two 6¼" squares of batting.
9. To form padded shape, place gold lamé, decorated side down, on a flat surface. Center both squares of batting, then cardboard, on gold lamé. Alternating sides and pulling fabric taut, use craft glue to glue edges of fabric to top (wrong side) of cardboard. Allow to dry.
10. Hot glue padded shape to lid. With center of cord at center top of shape, hot glue cord around shape. Tie ends of cord into a knot. Knot each streamer 1" from end and fray ends.

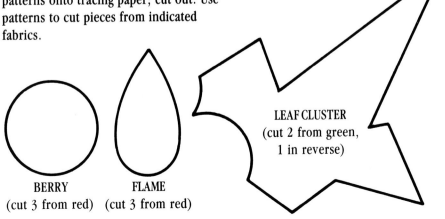

BERRY
(cut 3 from red)

FLAME
(cut 3 from red)

LEAF CLUSTER
(cut 2 from green,
1 in reverse)

SWEET CHEESE BALL

*F*eaturing a blend of chocolate, peppermint, and pecans, this sweet cheese ball is a creamy delight! To make your treat doubly delicious, give a friend a ready-to-eat Chocolate-Mint Cheese Ball to enjoy now and include a bag of the mix and instructions for making another one later. You'll want to add some chocolate wafers for serving, too.

CHOCOLATE-MINT CHEESE BALL MIX

- 1 package (12 ounces) semisweet chocolate chips
- 2 cups chopped pecans
- 1 cup 1-inch diameter peppermint candies (about thirty-six candies or 7 ounces)

In a blender or food processor, finely grind all ingredients. Place about 1½ cups mix into each of 4 separate resealable plastic bags. Give with recipe for making cheese ball.

Yield: about 6 cups mix, enough to make 4 cheese balls

To make cheese ball: Stir 1½ cups mix into one 8-ounce package softened cream cheese. Shape into a ball; wrap in plastic wrap and refrigerate until firm. To serve, let stand at room temperature 20 to 30 minutes or until softened. Serve with cookies.

Yield: 1 cheese ball

A Personal Touch

*P*ersonalized gifts are always special, and this versatile stenciled box is sure to be appreciated. It can be used year after year to hold holiday goodies, decorative arrangements, or even gifts! We filled this one with lots of yummy White Chocolate Popcorn Balls. Chunks of creamy white chocolate add a distinctive touch to these old-fashioned treats.

White Chocolate Popcorn Balls

    10 cups popped popcorn
     1 cup chopped pecans
     4 ounces white baking chocolate,
        coarsely chopped
    ½ cup butter or margarine
     4 cups miniature marshmallows

Combine popcorn, pecans, and chocolate in a large bowl. In a medium saucepan, melt butter over medium-low heat. Add marshmallows; stir constantly until marshmallows melt and mixture is smooth. Pour over popcorn mixture; toss until well coated. Dampen hands; shape mixture into 2½-inch balls. Cool completely on greased aluminum foil. Wrap each popcorn ball in cellophane or plastic wrap.

Yield: about 1½ dozen popcorn balls

Stenciled Box

You will need a wooden box; cream, red, dk red, green, and dk green acrylic paint; small round paintbrushes; 1¾"h purchased lettering stencil; acetate for holly stencil; permanent felt-tip pen with fine point; craft knife; cutting mat or a thick layer of newspapers; removable tape (optional); small stencil brushes; paper towels; fine sandpaper; and matte clear acrylic spray.

1. Allowing to dry between coats, paint box dk red.
2. To stencil family name on box, use lettering stencil and cream paint and follow Step 2 of Stenciling, page 122.
3. To stencil holly on box, use red paint for berries and green paint for leaves and follow Stenciling, page 122.
4. Use a pencil to write "the" above name. Use small round paintbrush and cream paint to paint over letters. Use small round paintbrush and dk green paint to paint veins and detail lines on holly leaves. Allow to dry.
5. Use sandpaper to remove some paint from edges of box.
6. Allowing to dry between coats, apply 2 coats of acrylic spray to box.

MONOGRAMMED TOFFEE

A personalized gift says "you're special," and each piece of Monogrammed Toffee echoes the thought. The luscious, buttery candy is coated with vanilla-flavored almond bark and initialed with decorating icing. Our monogrammed bag, made from a fingertip towel, is a distinctive way to present the toffee.

MONOGRAMMED TOFFEE

¾ cup butter

1 cup firmly packed brown sugar

8 ounces vanilla-flavored almond bark

Purchased green decorating icing

Stirring constantly, melt butter and sugar over medium heat in a small saucepan. Attach candy thermometer to pan, making sure thermometer does not touch bottom of pan. Stirring constantly, bring to a boil and continue to cook until syrup reaches hard crack stage (approximately 300 to 310 degrees). Test about ½ teaspoon syrup in ice water. Syrup should become brittle in ice water and remain brittle when removed from the water. For each toffee, spoon about 2 teaspoons syrup into ungreased 1¼-inch diameter candy molds. Cool completely. Invert molds and press on backs to release toffees.

Stirring constantly, melt almond bark over low heat in a small saucepan. Remove from heat. Using tongs, dip each piece of toffee in almond bark. Transfer to a wire rack with waxed paper underneath to cool completely. Use purchased green icing fitted with a small round tip to pipe desired initial on each piece of toffee. Allow icing to harden. Store in an airtight container.

Yield: about 4½ dozen toffees

MONOGRAMMED GIFT BAG

You will need an approx. 11" x 17" decorative fingertip towel (we used a towel with a cutwork border); a 3" fabric square for monogram appliqué; thread to match towel and thread to coordinate with fabric; 22" of 1"w satin ribbon; lightweight fusible interfacing; paper-backed fusible web; fabric paint for stencil; purchased 1" high lettering stencil; small stencil brush; paper towels; removable tape (optional); green, red, and black permanent felt-tip pens with fine points; and a compass.

1. For monogram appliqué, follow manufacturers' instructions to fuse interfacing, then web, to wrong side of fabric square. Use compass to draw a 2" dia. circle on fabric. Cut out circle.

2. Use lettering stencil and follow Step 2 of Stenciling, page 122, to stencil letter in center of fabric circle.

3. Referring to photo, use green pen to draw holly leaves around stenciled letter. Use red pen to draw berries. Use black pen to draw outlines and detail lines on leaves.

4. With wrong sides together, fold towel with decorated short edge extending 1" beyond plain short edge; press. Place towel on ironing board with decorated side (front of bag) up. With bottom of appliqué 2" above center of pressed edge (bottom of bag), fuse appliqué to towel. Using a medium width zigzag stitch with a very short stitch length and thread to coordinate with fabric, stitch over raw edge of appliqué.

5. For bag, match right sides and fold towel along pressed line (bottom of bag); press again. Using a ½" seam allowance and thread to match towel, sew sides of bag together. For bottom of bag, follow Step 4 of Fabric Bag instructions, page 122.

6. Place a plastic bag of toffee in bag; tie ribbon into a bow around top of bag.

*C*ross stitched with a merry little Christmas tree, this pretty holiday mug will give a friend many warm thoughts of you — especially when presented with a bag of Chocolate-Almond Coffee Mix. The flavors combined in the mix make it a triple-good treat. Just by adding hot water, your friend can enjoy this rich beverage anytime. Your gift is sure to be an instant hit!

HOCOLATE-ALMOND COFFEE IX

1 cup nondairy powdered coffee creamer
1 cup granulated sugar
½ cup instant coffee granules
½ cup cocoa
1 teaspoon almond extract

In a blender or food processor, finely ind all ingredients until well blended. ore in an airtight container. Give with rving instructions.

eld: about 2 cups coffee mix

o serve: Stir about 2 heaping teaspoons ffee mix into 6 ounces hot water.

For fabric bag, use an 8″ x 18″ fabric piece and follow Steps 2 and 4 of Fabric Bag instructions, page 122; press top edge of bag 1½″ to wrong side. Tie one 20″ length of 1″w ribbon and two 20″ lengths of ⅛″w ribbon into bows around top of bag. Tuck a sprig of artificial greenery behind bows.

CHRISTMAS TREE MUG

You will need a Crafter's Pride Stitch-A-Mug with Vinyl-Weave® (14 ct) insert and embroidery floss (see color key).

1. Follow manufacturer's instructions to remove insert from mug.

2. With design centered and bottom of design 1 fabric square from 1 long edge of insert, work design, repeating borders to within 1 fabric square of short edges. Use 2 strands of floss for Cross Stitch.

3. With short edges at back of mug, place insert in mug. Reassemble mug. Hand wash mug to protect stitchery.

CHRISTMAS TREE (36w x 48h)			
X	DMC	JPC	COLOR
★	434	5000	brown
▲	666	3046	red
V	701	6226	green
-	742	2303	gold
O	3326	3126	pink

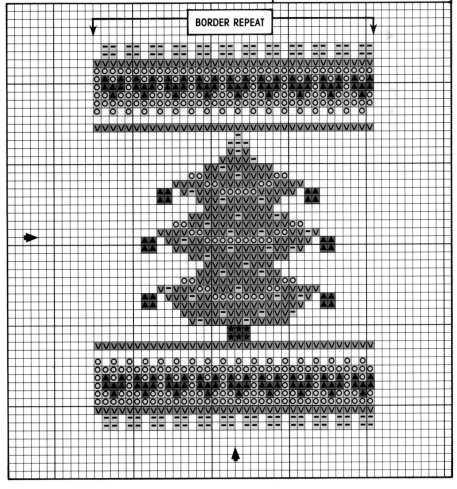

BORDER REPEAT

SANTA'S SNACK MIX

*H*oliday snackers will
joy this unusual trail mix!
etzels, toasted almonds,
d dried cranberries are
ven a sweet, crunchy
ating to create the crispy
ix. It's presented in a
ecious Santa tin that can
ld other goodies later.

UGARED CRANBERRY
RAIL MIX

1 cup whole almonds
2 cups small pretzels
1 cup dried cranberries (available at
    gourmet food stores)
1 egg white
½ cup granulated sugar
½ teaspoon ground cinnamon
½ teaspoon salt

Preheat oven to 350 degrees. Spread
monds evenly on an ungreased baking
eet. Bake 7 to 8 minutes or until nuts
e slightly darker in color. Cool
mpletely on pan.

Reduce oven temperature to
5 degrees. In a large bowl, combine
monds, pretzels, and cranberries. In a
all bowl, beat egg white until foamy.
ur over pretzel mixture; toss until
ell coated. In another small bowl,
mbine remaining ingredients. Sprinkle
er pretzel mixture; toss until well
ated. Spread evenly on a greased
king sheet. Bake 1 hour, stirring
ery 15 minutes. Cool completely on
n. Store in an airtight container.

eld: about 5 cups trail mix

SANTA TIN

You will need an 8″ dia. x 3¼″h tin
with lid, green spray paint, a 6″ square
of unbleached muslin fabric for face, a
9″ x 11″ piece of red fleece fabric for
hat, a 2¼″ x 26″ strip of fabric for
trim on tin, two 26″ lengths of ¼″w
jute braid trim, tracing paper, compass,
medium weight cardboard, polyester
fiberfill, two ³⁄₁₆″ dia. black beads for
eyes, ⅞″ dia. shank button for nose,
three 8″ lengths of ⅛″w ribbon,
⅝″ dia. jingle bell, white braided
wool doll hair for beard (available at
craft stores), cosmetic blush, fabric glue,
hot glue gun, glue sticks, and
transparent tape.

1. Paint tin and lid green; allow to dry.
2. With fabric strip centered on side of
tin, use fabric glue to glue strip to tin;
glue jute trim over top and bottom edges
of fabric strip. Allow to dry. Set tin
aside.
3. For Santa, use compass to draw a
4¼″ dia. circle on cardboard; draw a
5¼″ dia. circle on muslin. Cut out
circles.
4. For face, place muslin on a flat
surface. Place a handful of fiberfill at
center of muslin. Form fiberfill into an
approx. 4″ dia. mound. Center
cardboard circle over fiberfill. Pulling
fabric taut, use fabric glue to glue ½″
of edge of muslin to top (wrong side) of
cardboard circle. Allow to dry.
5. With padded side up, hot glue face to
center of lid.
6. For hat pattern, use hat top and
bottom patterns and follow Tracing
Patterns, page 122. Matching
registration marks (⊕), overlap top and
bottom patterns to form complete
pattern; tape patterns together.

7. Use pattern and cut 1 hat from hat
fabric. Trimming as necessary to make
edges lie flat, press long straight edges
of hat ½″ to wrong side; use fabric
glue to glue in place. Trim bottom
corners of hat even with bottom
(curved) edge of hat. Use fabric glue to
glue curved edge of hat to face. Hot
glue remainder of hat to lid.
8. Thread ribbon lengths through eye of
jingle bell; tie lengths together into a
bow. Hot glue bow and bell to point of
hat.
9. For beard, unbraid doll hair and cut
into 3½″ lengths. Hot glue lengths to
face.
10. Hot glue beads and button to face
for eyes and nose. Apply blush to
cheeks.

HAT TOP

HAT
BOTTOM

MERRY COOKIE KIT

*O*ne of Santa's little helpers will have a merry time with this cookie decorating kit! Baked in festive shapes, Potato Chip Cookies are all ready to be trimmed with the cookie sprinkles and icing included in the basket. To keep the job neat, there's an apron proclaiming "Elf at Work."

POTATO CHIP COOKIES

COOKIES
- 1 cup butter or margarine, softened
- 1 cup firmly packed brown sugar
- ½ cup granulated sugar
- 2 eggs
- 1 teaspoon vanilla extract
- 1 bag (7 ounces) potato chips, finely ground (about 2 cups)
- 3 cups all-purpose flour

ICING
- 4 cups confectioners sugar, sifted
- ½ cup milk
- Purchased colored sugars, sprinkles, and dragées to decorate

For cookies, cream butter and sugars until fluffy in a large bowl. Add eggs and vanilla; beat until smooth. Add potato chips and flour; stir until a soft dough forms. Cover and chill 30 minutes.

Preheat oven to 350 degrees. On a lightly floured surface, use a floured rolling pin to roll out dough to ¼-inch thickness. Use desired cookie cutters to cut out cookies. Transfer to a greased baking sheet. Bake 10 to 12 minutes or until edges are light brown. Transfer to

a wire rack to cool completely. Store in an airtight container.

For icing, stir sugar and milk together in a large bowl until smooth. Pour icing into an airtight container and store in refrigerator until ready to present. Give colored sugars, sprinkles, and dragées with cookies and icing.

Yield: about 5 dozen 3-inch cookies

COOKIE KIT

You will need a basket, craft ribbon, florist wire, excelsior, a child's red apron, 1¼" high white iron-on transfer letters, red and green dimensional fabric paint in squeeze bottles, three ⅝" dia. gold jingle bells, three 12" lengths each of 1/16"w green and 1/16"w white satin ribbon, thread to match apron, small jars, and red spray paint.

1. Wash, dry, and press apron according to fabric paint manufacturer recommendations.
2. For apron, use iron-on transfer letters and follow manufacturer's instructions to transfer "ELF AT WORK" onto apron. Use green paint to paint a line around each letter. Use red fabric paint to paint dots on letters that spell "ELF." Allow to dry.
3. Thread 1 length of each color of satin ribbon through eye of each jingle bell; tie ribbons together into bows. Tack bows to apron.
4. For jars, remove lids from jars and use spray paint to paint lids red. Allow to dry. Fill jars with cookie decorations.
5. For basket, form a multi-loop bow from craft ribbon; wire center of bow to secure. Wire bow to basket. Line basket with excelsior.

HELPFUL HOLIDAY BASKET

*D*uring the holidays
when drop-in visitors are
more frequent, a friend will
appreciate having this gift
basket on hand. Savory
Cheddar Spread is a smooth
blend of cheeses enhanced
with sherry and zesty spices.
Along with the spread,
include plates and napkins.
By simply adding crackers,
your friend will have a light
snack ready to share with
unexpected guests!

CHEDDAR SPREAD

2 cups (about 8 ounces) shredded
    sharp Cheddar cheese
1 package (8 ounces) cream cheese,
    softened
⅓ cup sherry
½ teaspoon garlic powder
½ teaspoon salt
¼ teaspoon ground white pepper
¼ teaspoon dry mustard

In a large bowl, combine all
ingredients until well blended using an
electric mixer. Transfer to an airtight
container and refrigerate 8 hours or
overnight to allow flavors to blend.
Store in refrigerator. Give with
instructions for serving.

Yield: about 2 cups spread

To serve: Let stand at room temperature
15 to 30 minutes or until softened.
Serve with crackers or bread.

For jar lid, follow Jar Lid Finishing,
page 122.

CREAMY PEACH EGGNOG

PEACH EGGNOG

1 quart prepared eggnog
3 cups half and half
1 can (12 ounces) apricot nectar
1 cup rum
1 cup peach-flavored brandy

In a 3-quart container, combine all ingredients; stir until well blended. Store in an airtight container in refrigerator. Serve chilled.

Yield: about fourteen 6-ounce servings

FRUITY COASTERS

For each coaster, you will need a 4″ square of 10 mesh plastic canvas, a #20 tapestry needle, Paternayan Persian yarn (see color key), a 3¾″ square of cork, ½ yd of ⅛″ dia. gold cord, and craft glue.

1. Follow chart and use Tent Stitch, Backstitch, and Overcast Stitch, page 123, to work coaster. Complete background with black Tent Stitches. Use 2 strands of yarn for Tent Stitch and Overcast Stitch and 1 for Backstitch.
2. Beginning at 1 corner of coaster and ½″ from 1 end of cord, glue cord to coaster. Glue ends to back of coaster.
3. Glue cork to coaster; allow to dry.

*L*aced with rum and peach brandy, this eggnog is a tasteful Yuletide offering. To accompany a bottle of the creamy Peach Eggnog, a set of plastic canvas needlepoint coasters features an elegant arrangement of fruit.

#220 black
#220 black (1 strand)
#300 dk purple
#301 purple
#334 lavender
#341 violet blue
#351 dk pink
#691 dk green
#692 green
#692 green (1 strand)
#773 yellow
#851 rust
#853 dk peach
#854 peach
#855 lt peach
#900 dk red
#948 vy lt pink
#968 red
#971 lt red

FRUITY COASTER (40 x 40 threads)

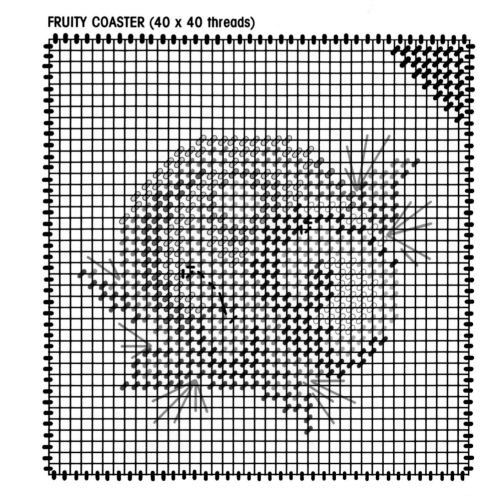

EASY JAM JARS

*H*ere's an easy-to-make gift that will bring Christmas cheer! A pleasing combination of purchased jam, amaretto, and nutmeg, Cheery Cherry Jam tastes as though it took hours (instead of minutes!) to prepare. The colorful jars of jam can be delivered in festive little baskets.

CHEERY CHERRY JAM

    2 jars (12 ounces each) cherry jam
        or preserves
    ¼ cup almond-flavored liqueur
    ½ teaspoon ground nutmeg

In a small saucepan, melt jam over low heat, stirring occasionally. Remove from heat; stir in remaining ingredients. Store in an airtight container in refrigerator.

Yield: about 1 pint jam

JAM JARS

For each jar, you will need green fabric to cover jar lid, lightweight cardboard, craft batting, craft glue, and ½"w red satin ribbon.

For each tag, you will need white paper, red print fabric, tracing paper, green felt-tip pen with medium point, 5" of ¹⁄₁₆" dia. gold cord and large needle (optional), and craft glue.

1. For jar lid insert, follow Jar Lid Finishing, page 122.

2. Trimming ribbon to fit, glue a length of ribbon around jar lid. Tie an 8" length of ribbon into a bow; cut V-shaped notches in ribbon ends. Glue bow to jar lid.

3. For tag, trace heart pattern onto tracing paper; cut out. Use pattern to cut 1 heart from white paper. Use pen to write desired words on heart. Glue a 3" square of fabric to a 3" square of paper; allow to dry. Glue heart to center of

fabric-covered paper. Trim fabric-covered paper to ¹⁄₈" larger than heart. Glue tag to jar lid, or use needle to thread gold cord through top center of tag and tie ends of cord around basket handle.

ZESTY ITALIAN CHEESE SNACKS

A cheese fancier will love these zesty treats! Garlic, oregano, and basil are blended with Cheddar cheese to create the Italian Cheese Snacks. Shaped in holiday candy molds, the savory tidbits are great with crackers or bread. To accompany the snacks, we painted a set of little wooden plates with a pinecone motif.

ITALIAN CHEESE SNACKS

    2 cups (about 8 ounces) shredded
        sharp Cheddar cheese
    1 teaspoon garlic powder
    ¼ teaspoon dried oregano leaves,
        crushed
    ¼ teaspoon dried basil leaves,
        crushed

In the top of a double boiler, combine all ingredients. Stirring constantly, cook over boiling water until cheese melts. Remove from heat, leaving cheese mixture over hot water. For each cheese snack, spoon about ½ teaspoon cheese mixture into ungreased 1-inch candy molds. Cover and refrigerate until firm. To remove cheese snacks from candy molds, use a sharp knife to loosen edges. Invert molds and press on backs to release cheese snacks. Wrap in plastic wrap and store in refrigerator until ready to present. Serve with bread or crackers. Include serving suggestions with gift.

Yield: about 3 dozen cheese snacks

PINECONE PLATES

For each plate, you will need an unfinished wooden plate (available at craft stores), tracing paper, graphite transfer paper, brown permanent felt tip pen with fine point, green and brown liquid fabric dye, small round paintbrushes, and clear polyurethane spray.

Note: Plates are for decorative use and should only be used for dry foods. Wipe clean with a damp cloth.

1. Trace pattern onto tracing paper.
2. Use transfer paper to transfer pattern to plate.
3. Use brown pen to draw over lines of designs.
4. Use dye to paint pinecones brown and greenery green. Allow to dry.
5. Allowing to dry between coats, apply 2 coats of polyurethane spray to plate.

AN ELEGANT GIFT

*R*ichly hued wrapping paper, a glistening bow, and an artful arrangement of fruit and ivy transform a cardboard beverage carton into an elegant carrier for these Peach Wine Coolers. Topped with gold foil, the ''recycled'' beverage bottles are just right for holding the delicately flavored drink.

PEACH WINE COOLERS

  1 package (16 ounces) frozen unsweetened peaches, thawed
  1 quart peach juice
  1 bottle (750 ml) dry white wine
  1 can (12 ounces) apricot nectar
  1 cup granulated sugar

In a blender or food processor, purée peaches. In a 3-quart container, combine peaches and remaining ingredients. Cover and chill 8 hours or overnight to allow flavors to blend. Store in refrigerator. Serve chilled.

Yield: about thirteen 6-ounce servings

Note: If making cooler carrier, save a cardboard bottled drink carrier and empty bottles. When ready to present, fill washed bottles with wine coolers, screw on lids, and press gold foil candy wrappers (available at cooking supply stores) around tops of bottles.

COOLER CARRIER

You will need a cardboard bottled drink carrier, gold spray paint, desired wrapping paper, spray adhesive, craft knife, cutting mat or a thick layer of newspapers, ⅝"w gold ribbon, miniature artificial fruit, artificial ivy, florist wire, hot glue gun, and glue sticks.

1. Paint carrier gold; allow to dry.
2. Measure height of side of carrier at tallest point; add ½". Measure around sides of carrier; add ½". Cut wrapping paper the determined measurements. Cut a length from ribbon the same length as paper.
3. With 1 long edge extending ¼" beyond bottom edge of carrier and overlapping short edges, use spray adhesive to glue wrapping paper to side of carrier; fold bottom edge of paper to bottom of carrier and press in place.
4. Place carrier on cutting mat and use craft knife to trim top edge of paper even with top edge of carrier.
5. Hot glue ribbon length around carrier approx. ¼" from top edge.
6. Form a multi-loop bow from ribbon; wrap wire around bow at center to secure.
7. Arrange bow, fruit, and ivy at 1 corner and on handle of carrier; use hot glue to secure.

Coffee Lover's Candy

Chocolate-Covered Espresso Beans will delight coffee lover! Crunchy espresso beans are coated with rich dark chocolate to create these exquisite candies. They're perfect for serving after dinner or with coffee. You can present the foil-wrapped candies in a single mug or with a set of four a holiday basket.

Chocolate-Covered Espresso Beans

9 ounces semisweet baking
    chocolate, chopped
1 rounded tablespoon espresso
    beans

Place espresso beans about 1 inch apart on a piece of aluminum foil. In a small saucepan, melt chocolate over low heat, stirring constantly, until smooth. Spoon about ½ teaspoon chocolate over each espresso bean. Cool completely. Store in an airtight container in a cool, dry place. If desired, wrap each candy in a foil wrapper.

Yield: about 5 dozen candies

A JOYOUS BREAKFAST SPREAD

JOYOUS NOEL ORNAMENT

You will need a 7″ square of white Aida (14 ct), a 7″ fabric square for backing, thread to match fabric, 23″ of ⅛″ dia. red twisted satin cord, embroidery floss (see color key), polyester fiberfill, and fabric glue.

1. Using 2 strands of floss for Cross Stitch and Backstitch, work design on Aida.
2. Place stitched piece and backing fabric right sides together. Stitching ⅜″ from stitched design and leaving an opening for turning, sew stitched piece and backing fabric together. Trim seam allowance and cut corners diagonally. Turn right side out and press. Stuff ornament with fiberfill. Sew final closure by hand.
3. Glue ½″ at 1 end of cord to top back of ornament; glue cord to edge of ornament over seamline. Glue ½″ of remaining end of cord to top back of ornament, forming a hanging loop. Allow to dry. Tie a knot in hanging loop close to top of ornament.

A sweet combination cream cheese, strawberry reserves, and chopped ans makes Strawberry read a delectable substitute butter on bread or ffins. To add holiday er to a friend's breakfast, k a crock of the spread in imple basket and include r cross-stitched ornament.

RAWBERRY SPREAD

1 package (8 ounces) cream cheese, softened
1 jar (10 ounces) strawberry jam or preserves
1 teaspoon dried grated orange peel
1 cup finely chopped pecans

In a medium bowl, combine cream eese, jam, and orange peel. Stir in cans. Cover and chill until firm. Store an airtight container in refrigerator. rve with toast or muffins. Include rving suggestions with gift.

eld: about 3 cups spread

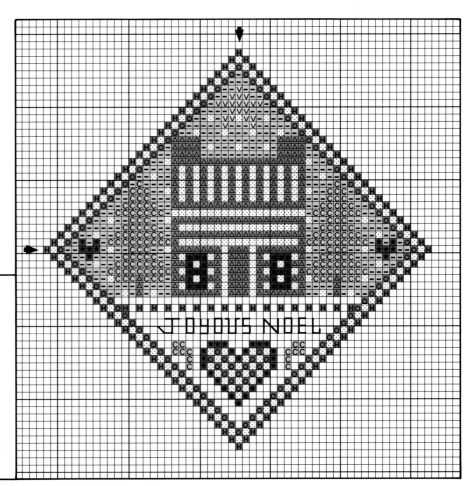

JOYOUS NOEL (55w x 55h)			
X	DMC	B'ST	JPC	COLOR
	blanc		1001	white
✱	300			brown
	310	╱	8403	black
o	321		3500	red
△	435		5371	tan
−	517		7162	blue
V	676		2305	lt gold
★	816		3410	dk red
H	895		6021	dk green
C	987		6258	green

WINTER WARMER DINNER PARTY

A cozy dinner party is just the thing to ward off winter's chill! To set the mood, this charming table features a frosty family of snowpeople enjoying a sledding expedition. (Instructions for the snowpeople are given on page 52.) Three boldly checked mufflers placed across the table serve as place mats for the six settings of old-fashioned enamelware. The cups, personalized with shiny dimensional paint, make darling favors for your guests to keep. The napkins and utensils are tucked inside bright red mittens — so each couple will have a pair for the lady to wear home. With these clever decorating ideas and our hearty menu, your gathering is sure to be a warming experience.

Turkey Nachos

Pumpkin Soup

Deep-Dish Vegetable Pie

Oatmeal-Rye Rolls

Glazed Lemon Cheesecake

Honey-of-a-Punch

PUMPKIN SOUP

Pumpkin Soup may be served in a hollowed-out pumpkin.

> 1 pound cooked smoked sausage (such as kielbasa), cut into ½-inch slices
> 1 tablespoon butter or margarine
> 1 tablespoon vegetable oil
> ¼ cup all-purpose flour
> 1 pound stew meat, cut into 1-inch cubes
> 1½ cups chopped onion (about 3 medium onions)
> ⅔ cup chopped celery (about 2 ribs celery)
> 5 cups water
> 1½ cups thinly sliced carrots (about 2 large carrots)
> ½ teaspoon dried thyme
> 1½ teaspoons salt
> ¼ teaspoon ground black pepper
> 1 bay leaf
> 2½ cups ½-inch cubes of peeled pumpkin (cut from top of pumpkin) or winter squash

Place sausage in a large saucepan and add enough water to cover sausage. Bring to a boil and cook 3 minutes; drain and set aside. In a Dutch oven, heat butter and oil over medium heat. Sprinkle flour over stew meat. Add stew meat to butter mixture and cook, stirring occasionally, until meat browns. Add onion and celery; cook until tender. Add sausage and next 6 ingredients; stir until well blended. Bring to a boil; reduce heat to low, cover, and simmer about 1 hour. Add pumpkin and cook about 30 minutes or until pumpkin is tender. Remove bay leaf. Serve hot.

Yield: about 10 servings

This robust soup offers a tasty new way to prepare fresh pumpkin! Packed with chunks of beef and sausage along with pumpkin and other vegetables, Pumpkin Soup is a satisfying first course or entrée.

URKEY NACHOS

1 can (16 ounces) regular or
    vegetarian refried beans
1 teaspoon chili powder
1 teaspoon ground cumin
2 tablespoons vegetable oil
1 pound cooked turkey breast,
    diced (about 3½ cups)
½ cup chopped onion (about
    1 medium onion)
1 can (4 ounces) chopped mild
    green chilies
2 tablespoons chopped fresh
    cilantro leaves
1 teaspoon salt
½ teaspoon ground black pepper
1 cup finely chopped tomato (about
    1 large tomato)
1 bag (10½ ounces) round tortilla
    chips
2 cups (about 8 ounces) shredded
    Monterey Jack cheese

In a small saucepan, combine beans,
ili powder, and cumin. Cook, stirring
casionally, over medium-low heat
til heated through. Remove from heat
d cover.

In a large skillet, heat oil over
edium heat. Add turkey, onion,
ilies, cilantro, salt, and pepper.
ok, stirring occasionally, until onion
 tender. Remove from heat and stir in
mato.

Preheat oven to 425 degrees. Spread
out 1 teaspoon bean mixture evenly
er each tortilla chip; place in a single
yer on a greased baking sheet. Spoon
out 1 tablespoon turkey mixture over
an mixture. Sprinkle cheese evenly
er turkey mixture. Bake 5 to
 minutes or until cheese melts. Serve
arm.

eld: about 4½ dozen nachos

OATMEAL-RYE ROLLS

2 cups water
1 cup old-fashioned rolled oats
3 cups all-purpose flour
2 cups whole-wheat flour
1 cup rye flour
½ cup nonfat dry milk
2½ teaspoons salt
2 packages rapid-rising dry yeast
⅓ cup warm water
½ cup honey
¼ cup vegetable oil
    Vegetable cooking spray

In a medium saucepan, bring 2 cups
water to a boil over high heat. Remove
from heat; stir in oats. Cool to room
temperature.

In a large bowl, sift together flours,
dry milk, and salt. In a small bowl,
dissolve yeast in ⅓ cup warm water.
Add oats mixture, yeast mixture, honey,
and oil to dry ingredients. Stir until a
soft dough forms. Turn onto a lightly
floured surface and knead until dough
becomes smooth and elastic. Place in a
large bowl sprayed with cooking spray,
turning once to coat top of dough.
Cover and let rise in a warm place
(80 to 85 degrees) 1 hour or until
doubled in size. Turn dough onto a
lightly floured surface and punch down.
Shape dough into 2-inch balls and place
2 inches apart on a greased baking
sheet. Spray tops of rolls with cooking
spray, cover, and let rise in a warm
place 1 hour or until doubled in size.

Preheat oven to 350 degrees. Bake
25 to 30 minutes or until golden brown.
Serve warm or cool completely on a
wire rack.

Yield: about 2 dozen rolls

*Bite-size Turkey Nachos make
spicy little appetizers.*

HONEY-OF-A-PUNCH

5 cups unsweetened pineapple juice
5 cups cranberry juice cocktail
2 cups water
1 cup honey
2 tablespoons whole allspice
4 two-inch cinnamon sticks

Place first 4 ingredients in a large
Dutch oven. Place allspice and
cinnamon sticks in center of a 6-inch
square of cheesecloth and tie with
string. Add spices to punch mixture and
simmer over medium-low heat 1 hour.
Serve hot. (Punch may also be prepared
by placing first 4 ingredients in a large
electric percolator. Stir until well
blended. Place allspice and cinnamon
sticks in percolator basket. Perk
through complete cycle.)

Yield: about seventeen 6-ounce servings

GLAZED LEMON CHEESECAKE

Glazed Lemon Cheesecake must be made at least 1 day in advance.

CRUST

- 2½ cups graham cracker crumbs
- 10 tablespoons butter or margarine, melted
- ¼ cup granulated sugar

FILLING

- 3 packages (8 ounces each) cream cheese, softened
- 1¼ cups granulated sugar
- 4 eggs
- 4 tablespoons fresh lemon juice
- 1 tablespoon freshly grated lemon peel
- 1 teaspoon lemon extract

GLAZE

- 3 tablespoons fresh lemon juice
- 1 tablespoon cornstarch
- 1 jar (10 ounces) seedless raspberry jam or preserves

Preheat oven to 350 degrees. For crust, combine all ingredients in a medium bowl. Press into bottom and 2 inches up sides of a greased 9-inch springform pan. Bake 5 minutes. Cool completely on a wire rack.

For filling, beat cream cheese and sugar in a large bowl until fluffy using an electric mixer. Add eggs, one at a time, beating well after each addition. Add remaining ingredients; beat until well blended. Pour filling into crust. Bake 50 to 55 minutes or until set in center. Turn off oven. Leaving door slightly open, leave cheesecake in oven 1 hour. Cool completely on a wire rack. Remove sides of pan.

For glaze, stir lemon juice and cornstarch together to make a thin paste. Melt jam in a small saucepan over low heat. Stirring constantly, add cornstarch mixture and cook over medium heat until mixture thickens slightly. Cool to room temperature. Spread glaze evenly over top of cake. Cover and refrigerate 8 hours or overnight.

Yield: about 16 servings

SNOWPEOPLE

For each large snowperson, you will need one 5″ and one 4″ dia. plastic foam ball, 2 approx. ¼″w rocks for eyes, 3 approx. ½″w rocks for buttons, 2 approx. 4½″ long twigs for arms, a 4″ x 22″ strip of fabric for neck scarf, and a 10″ x 19″ piece of red felt for head scarf or a 3½″ dia. black felt hat (available at craft stores).

For each medium snowperson, you will need one 4″ and one 3″ dia. plastic foam ball, 2 approx. ¼″w rocks for eyes, 3 approx. ½″w rocks for buttons, 2 approx. 3″ long twigs for arms, a 3″ x 18″ strip of fabric for neck scarf, and a 5″ x 16″ piece of red felt for head scarf or a 3½″ dia. black felt hat (available at craft stores).

For each small snowperson, you will need one 2½″ and one 2″ dia. plastic foam ball, 2 approx. ⅛″w rocks for eyes, 3 approx. ⅜″w rocks for buttons, 2 approx. 2½″ long twigs for arms, a 2″ x 15″ strip of fabric for neck scarf, and a 2″ dia. black felt hat (available at craft stores).

You will also need instant papier mâché (we used Celluclay® Instant Papier Mâché); resealable plastic bag (optional); gesso; white, orange, and black acrylic paint; foam brushes; small round paintbrush; hot glue gun; glue sticks; a toothpick; paring knife; and matte clear acrylic spray.

1. Use knife to cut ¼″ from 1 side of large plastic foam ball (body), forming flat surface (bottom).

2. Insert 1″ of toothpick into small plastic foam ball (head). Centering small ball on top of large ball, insert toothpick into large ball.

3. Follow manufacturer's instructions mix papier mâché with water. Excess mixture can be stored in a resealable plastic bag in refrigerator for up to 4 days.

4. Keeping fingers wet while working, apply a ⅛″ to ¼″ thick layer of papier mâché over head and body. For nose on large or medium snowperson form a 1″ long cone shape with a ½″ dia. base from a small piece of papier mâché. For nose on small snowperson, form a ¾″ long cone shape with a ⅜″ dia. base. Press base of cone shape onto head; smooth edge of cone shape onto head to secure. For arms, push end of 1 twig ½″ into body at each side. Allow to dry.

5. Apply 1 coat of gesso and 1 coat of white paint to head and body, allowing to dry between coats. Paint nose orange and rocks black; allow to dry.

6. Glue small rocks to head for eyes; glue large rocks to body for buttons.

7. Apply 1 coat of acrylic spray to snowperson; allow to dry.

8. For neck scarf, fringe short edges of fabric strip ½″. Matching wrong sides, press long edges of strip to center. Tie scarf around neck.

9. For hat, glue hat to head. For head scarf, cut felt piece from each corner of 1 long edge to center of remaining long edge to form a triangle. Tie scarf around head.

This fresh Spinach-Peach Salad features sweet red onion and a tangy poppy seed dressing. Our painted wooden bowl is great for carrying the salad to holiday potlucks — and it makes a festive hostess gift, too.

SPINACH-PEACH SALAD

DRESSING

⅓ cup mayonnaise
¼ cup orange juice
1 teaspoon granulated sugar
1 teaspoon poppy seeds

SALAD

6 cups (about 10 ounces) fresh spinach, torn into bite-size pieces
1 cup sliced red onion (about 1 medium onion)
1 can (29 ounces) peach slices, drained

For dressing, stir together all ingredients until well blended. Set aside.

For salad, toss together spinach, onion, and peaches in a large bowl. Cover and refrigerate salad and dressing in separate containers until ready to serve.

To serve, pour dressing over salad; toss until well coated.

Yield: about 12 servings

POINSETTIA SALAD BOWL

You will need a pre-finished wooden salad bowl with sides at least 4½″ high; tracing paper; graphite transfer paper; black permanent felt tip pen with fine point; gold, dk gold, red, lt green, and green acrylic paint; small round paintbrushes; fine sandpaper; and clear polyurethane spray.

Note: To clean bowl after use, hand wash with mild soap and water.

1. Lightly sand area of bowl to be painted.
2. Trace pattern, page 112, onto tracing paper.
3. Use transfer paper to transfer pattern to bowl.
4. Use pen to draw over transferred lines.
5. For each color of paint, mix 2 parts paint to 1 part water. Allowing to dry between colors, paint flower center gold with dk gold shading, petals red, leaves lt green with green shading, and tendrils green.
6. Allowing to dry between coats, apply 2 coats of polyurethane spray to painted area of bowl.

Rosemary Tea has a refreshing, distinctive flavor. Cream cheese pastry and a rich, sweet filling make Buttermilk Pecan Pies extra special.

BUTTERMILK PECAN PIES

CRUST

- 1 cup plus 1 tablespoon all-purpose flour
- ½ cup butter or margarine, softened
- 1 package (3 ounces) cream cheese, softened

FILLING

- ¾ cup granulated sugar
- 1 egg
- ⅓ cup buttermilk
- 3 tablespoons butter or margarine, melted
- 1 tablespoon all-purpose flour
- ¼ teaspoon salt
- ¾ cup chopped pecans

For crust, stir all ingredients together in a medium bowl. Shape dough into twenty-four 1-inch balls. Press balls of dough into bottoms and up sides of greased miniature muffin pans.

Preheat oven to 350 degrees. For filling, beat sugar and egg together in a medium bowl. Add next 4 ingredients; beat until smooth. Stir in pecans. Spoon filling into crusts, filling each tin. Bake 30 to 35 minutes or until golden brown. Cool in pans 5 minutes. Transfer to a wire rack to cool completely. Store in an airtight container.

Yield: 2 dozen pies

TEAPOT COOKIES

COOKIES

- 1 cup butter or margarine, softene
- 1½ cups granulated sugar
- 1 egg
- 1 teaspoon vanilla extract
- 2¾ cups all-purpose flour
- ¼ teaspoon salt

ICING

- 3¾ cups confectioners sugar, sifted
- 9 tablespoons milk
- ½ teaspoon almond extract
  Pink paste food coloring
  Purchased white decorating icin
  Silver dragées

For cookies, preheat oven to 375 degrees. In a large bowl, cream butter and sugar until fluffy. Add egg and vanilla; beat until smooth. Add flour and salt; stir until a soft dough forms. Trace teapot pattern, page 118 onto tracing paper; cut out. On a light floured surface, use a floured rolling pin to roll out dough to ⅛-inch thickness. Place pattern on dough and use a sharp knife to cut out cookies. U a drinking straw to make a hole in top of each cookie. Transfer to a greased baking sheet. Bake 8 to 10 minutes or until edges are light brown. Transfer t a wire rack with waxed paper underneath to cool completely.

For icing, stir together sugar, milk, and almond extract in a medium bowl until smooth. Tint icing pink and ice cookies. Allow icing to harden. Transf purchased decorating icing to a pastry bag fitted with a very small round tip. Refer to photo, page 54, and pipe icin on cookies. Decorate with dragées. Allow icing to harden. Store in an airtight container until ready to decora tree.

Yield: about 4 dozen cookies

PEACHES AND CREAM SOUFFLÉS

Soufflés and topping should be made ... day in advance.

SOUFFLÉS

- 8 egg yolks
- 1 cup granulated sugar
- 1 package (16 ounces) frozen unsweetened peaches, thawed and puréed
- 2 tablespoons peach schnapps (optional)
- ½ cup apricot nectar
- 2 envelopes unflavored gelatin
- 3 cups whipping cream

TOPPING

- 1 package (16 ounces) frozen unsweetened peaches, thawed and coarsely chopped
- 1 cup granulated sugar
- ¼ cup peach schnapps (optional)

For soufflés, beat egg yolks and sugar until creamy in a medium bowl using an electric mixer. Stir in peaches. If desired, stir in schnapps. In a large saucepan, combine apricot nectar and gelatin. Cook over low heat, stirring until gelatin is dissolved. Stir peach mixture into gelatin mixture, mixing well. Stirring constantly, cook over medium heat until mixture begins to boil. Remove from heat and cool to room temperature.

Place a large bowl and beaters from electric mixer in refrigerator until well chilled. In chilled bowl, whip cream until stiff. Fold whipped cream into peach mixture. Spoon into teacups, filling each ¾ full. Cover and refrigerate until firm.

For topping, combine peaches and sugar in a medium saucepan; bring to a boil. Cook about 15 minutes or until sauce thickens slightly. Remove from heat. If desired, stir in schnapps. Cover and refrigerate until chilled. To serve, spoon about 1 tablespoon topping over each soufflé.

Yield: eighteen 4-ounce soufflés

Light and fluffy, Peaches and Cream Soufflés are topped with a peachy sauce. Your treasured teacups are perfect for serving the little desserts.

ROSEMARY TEA

- ½ cup tea leaves
- 1 tablespoon dried rosemary leaves

In a blender or food processor, finely grind tea and rosemary. Store in an airtight container.

To brew tea, place 1 teaspoon tea for each 8 ounces of water in a warm teapot. Bring water to a rolling boil and pour over tea. Steep tea 5 minutes, stir, and strain through cheesecloth. Serve hot or over ice.

Yield: about ⅓ cup tea leaves

SILVER BELLS PUNCH

- 1 can (46 ounces) unsweetened pineapple juice, chilled
- 2 cups piña colada drink mixer, chilled
- 1 can (12 ounces) frozen orange juice concentrate, thawed
- 1 liter club soda, chilled
- 1 liter lemon-lime soft drink, chilled
- 1 package (10 ounces) frozen raspberries in syrup, slightly thawed

In a punch bowl, stir together first 5 ingredients. To serve, stir in raspberries. Serve chilled.

Yield: about twenty-four 6-ounce servings

SPINACH-ARTICHOKE CASSEROLE

CRUST

- 1½ cups all-purpose flour
- ½ cup butter or margarine, softened
- 1 package (3 ounces) cream cheese, softened
- ½ teaspoon salt

FILLING

- 4 eggs
- 1 cup milk
- 1 cup all-purpose flour
- 3 tablespoons butter or margarine, melted
- 1 tablespoon baking powder
- 1 teaspoon dried basil leaves
- 1 teaspoon salt
- ½ teaspoon ground black pepper
- ½ teaspoon garlic powder
- 1 can (14 ounces) artichoke hearts, drained and chopped
- 1 package (10 ounces) frozen chopped spinach, thawed and well drained
- 2 cups (about 8 ounces) shredded Swiss cheese
- 1½ cups finely chopped onion (about 2 large onions)

Preheat oven to 350 degrees. For crust, combine all ingredients in a medium bowl. Press dough into bottom and 1 inch up sides of a greased 9 x 13-inch glass baking dish. Prick bottom of crust with a fork. Bake 10 minutes. Remove from oven.

For filling, mix first 9 ingredients in a large bowl until well blended using an electric mixer. Stir in remaining ingredients. Pour mixture

This cheesy Spinach-Artichoke Casserole will please the Christmas crowd. Our padded casserole carrier is a festive way to keep your dish warm.

into crust. Bake 35 to 40 minutes or until set in center. Cut into squares and serve hot.

Yield: 10 to 12 servings

CASSEROLE CARRIER

You will need two 15½" x 19½" pieces of fabric, thread to match fabric, two 15½" x 19½" pieces of low-loft polyester bonded batting, four ⅞" dia. jingle bells, and four 12" lengths of ¼"w ribbon.

1. Place batting pieces together. Place fabric pieces right sides together on top of batting pieces. Leaving an opening for turning, use a ½" seam allowance and stitch all layers together. Clip corners diagonally, turn right side out, and press; sew final closure by hand.
2. Stitch 3" from each edge of carrier.
3. Fold fabric up along stitched lines, matching lines to form each corner. Tack sides together at each corner.
4. Thread 1 ribbon length through eye of each jingle bell. Tie each ribbon length into a bow; trim ends. Tack 1 bow and jingle bell at each corner of carrier.

These luscious dessert squares are sure to be enjoyed! They feature a creamy pumpkin and spice cheesecake layered between a nutty graham cracker crust and a rich praline topping.

PUMPKIN CHEESECAKE SQUARES

CRUST
- 1 cup graham cracker crumbs
- ½ cup walnuts, finely ground
- ¼ cup granulated sugar
- ½ teaspoon pumpkin pie spice
- ¼ teaspoon ground cinnamon
- ¼ teaspoon ground nutmeg
- ¼ cup butter or margarine, melted

FILLING
- 12 ounces cream cheese, softened
- ¾ cup firmly packed brown sugar
- 3 eggs
- ¾ cup canned pumpkin
- ½ teaspoon orange extract
- ½ teaspoon ground cinnamon
- ½ teaspoon pumpkin pie spice
- ¼ teaspoon ground nutmeg

TOPPING
- 1 cup butter or margarine
- 1 cup firmly packed brown sugar
- ½ teaspoon pumpkin pie spice
- 1½ cups chopped walnuts

For crust, combine first 6 ingredients in a large bowl. Add butter; stir until mixture is crumbly. Press into bottom of a greased 9 x 13-inch glass baking dish.

Preheat oven to 350 degrees. For filling, mix cream cheese and sugar in a large bowl until fluffy using an electric mixer. Add remaining ingredients; beat until well blended. Pour over crust. Bake 55 to 60 minutes or until set in center. Cool completely on a wire rack.

For topping, combine first 3 ingredients in a medium saucepan. Stirring constantly, cook over medium heat until sugar dissolves. Bring to a boil and cook 2 to 3 minutes or until syrup thickens. Stir in walnuts. Pour over cooled filling. Cool completely. Cover and refrigerate until ready to serve. Cut into squares to serve. Store in refrigerator.

Yield: about 2 dozen squares

Creamy, delicately flavored Shrimp Spread (top) is delicious served with crackers. Sausage-Cream Cheese Squares have a flaky crust that's easy to make with refrigerated crescent roll dough. Featuring no-sew appliqués, the napkins harmonize nicely with the table runner shown on the next page.

GRASSHOPPER PIE

CRUST

   30 chocolate wafer cookies
   ¼ cup butter or margarine, melted

FILLING

   30 large marshmallows
   ½ cup milk
   ¼ cup crème de menthe
   1 cup whipping cream
      Green food coloring (optional)

   14 Andes® chocolate mint wafer candies for garnish

For crust, preheat oven to 350 degrees. In a blender or food processor, finely grind cookies. With food processor running, slowly add melted butter; process until well blended. Press crumb mixture into bottom and up sides of a 9-inch pie pan. Bake crust 7 minutes. Cool completely on a wire rack.

For filling, place a medium bowl and beaters from an electric mixer in refrigerator until well chilled. In the top of a double boiler, combine marshmallows and milk. Stirring frequently, cook over hot, not boiling water until smooth. Remove from heat and pour into a large bowl. Cool to room temperature. Stir in crème de menthe.

In chilled bowl, whip cream until soft peaks form. Fold whipped cream into marshmallow mixture. If desired, tint green. Spoon evenly into cooled crust. Loosely cover and refrigerate until set. Garnish with chocolate mint candies.

Yield: about 8 servings

SHRIMP SPREAD

Shrimp Spread should be made 1 day in advance.

   1½ pounds cooked and peeled shrimp
   1 package (8 ounces) cream cheese, softened
   ¼ cup finely chopped onion
   2 tablespoons sour cream
   2 teaspoons sweet pickle relish
   1½ teaspoons Dijon-style mustard
   1½ teaspoons hot pepper sauce
      Crackers or bread to serve

Reserve several shrimp for garnish. Finely chop remaining shrimp. In a large bowl, combine chopped shrimp, cream cheese, onion, sour cream, pickle relish, mustard, and hot pepper sauce; stir until well blended. Cover and refrigerate 8 hours or overnight to allow flavors to blend. Garnish with reserved shrimp. Serve with crackers or bread.

Yield: about 4 cups spread

SAUSAGE-CREAM CHEESE SQUARES

2 cans (8 ounces each)
  refrigerated crescent rolls
2 packages (8 ounces each) cream
  cheese, softened
½ teaspoon dried basil leaves,
  crushed
¼ teaspoon garlic powder
½ pounds mild pork sausage,
  cooked, drained, and crumbled
12 ounces provolone cheese,
  shredded (about 3 cups)
¾ cup finely chopped sweet red
  pepper

Preheat oven to 350 degrees. Unroll
can of crescent roll dough onto a
greased baking sheet, being careful not
to separate dough into pieces. Press
dough into an 8 x 13-inch rectangle.
Using a second greased baking sheet,
repeat for remaining can of rolls. Bake
to 15 minutes or until golden brown.
Remove from oven.
In a medium bowl, combine next
ingredients. Spread cream cheese
mixture evenly over baked dough.
Sprinkle remaining ingredients evenly
over cream cheese mixture. Bake 5 to
minutes or until cheese melts. Cut into
inch squares and serve warm.

Yield: about 4 dozen appetizers

CHOCOLATE SNOWBALL COOKIES

½ cups (9 ounces) semisweet
  chocolate chips
1 package (8 ounces) cream cheese,
  cut into small pieces
½ teaspoons vanilla extract
3 cups finely ground chocolate
  wafer cookies (about
  64 cookies)

Served warm, Chocolate Eggnog is a wonderful variation of the traditional beverage. No-bake Chocolate Snowball Cookies are coated with confectioners sugar. A ready-made table runner is dressed up with musical appliqués, and purchased caroling books are given festive holiday covers.

1 cup finely ground pecans
  Confectioners sugar, sifted

In a large saucepan, melt chocolate
chips over low heat, stirring constantly.
Add cream cheese and vanilla, stirring
until smooth. Remove from heat. Stir in
cookie crumbs and pecans. Shape into
1-inch balls; roll in confectioners sugar.
Cover and refrigerate 8 hours or until
firm. Roll in confectioners sugar again.
Store in an airtight container in
refrigerator.

Yield: about 6 dozen cookies

CRANBERRY-CHAMPAGNE COCKTAILS

- 1 quart cranberry juice cocktail, chilled
- 1 bottle (750 ml) champagne, chilled

Combine cranberry juice and champagne in a 2-quart pitcher; stir until well blended. Serve chilled.

Yield: about nine 6-ounce servings

CHOCOLATE EGGNOG

- 1 quart prepared eggnog
- ½ cup chocolate syrup
- ¼ teaspoon ground nutmeg
- 1 tablespoon vanilla extract
  Ground nutmeg for garnish

In a large saucepan, combine eggnog, chocolate syrup, and ¼ teaspoon nutmeg. Stirring occasionally, cook over medium-low heat 20 to 25 minutes or until heated through (do not boil). Remove from heat; stir in vanilla. To serve, pour into cups; sprinkle tops lightly with nutmeg. Serve warm.

Yield: six 6-ounce servings

EVERGREEN CENTERPIECE

For our centerpiece, we started with a purchased S-shaped greenery swag decorated with pinecones and spritzed with gold metallic paint. In the swag, we arranged a hurricane lamp and purchased nutcracker and musical motif ornaments, using hot glue to secure the ornaments in place. A bow made from 2½" wide wired ribbon was wired to one end of the swag. For added color and shine, lengths of ⅜" wide red satin ribbon and ⅛" diameter metallic cord were wound among the branches of greenery.

TABLE RUNNER AND COCKTAIL NAPKINS

You will need gold lamé fabric, lightweight fusible interfacing, paper-backed fusible web, iridescent gold dimensional fabric paint in a squeeze bottle, and tracing paper.

For table runner, you will also need a purchased table runner (ours measures 12½" x 72"), ½"w gold metallic ribbon, and fabric glue.

For each cocktail napkin, you will also need a 10" fabric square, purchased bias binding, and thread to match binding.

1. For table runner, wash, dry, and press table runner according to paint manufacturer's recommendations.
2. For appliqués, follow manufacturers' instructions to fuse interfacing, then web, to wrong side of lamé fabric.
3. Trace music motif patterns, page 112, onto tracing paper and cut out. Use patterns to cut desired music motifs from lamé fabric.
4. (*Note:* Refer to photo, page 65, for Steps 4 - 6.) Fuse motifs to table runner.
5. Centering lines of paint over raw edges of appliqués, paint over edges of appliqués; paint detail lines. Allow to dry.
6. For ribbon trim, glue ribbon lengths along edges of runner, mitering lengths at corners.
7. For each cocktail napkin, refer to photo, page 64, and follow Steps 1 - 5 to appliqué desired music motif on 1 corner of fabric square.
8. Apply bias binding to edge of fabric square.
9. To launder table runner or cocktail napkins, follow paint manufacturer's recommendations.

SONGBOOK FAVORS

For each favor, you will need a purchased songbook (available at mu stores), red construction paper or wrapping paper, plaid fabric, ½"w gold metallic ribbon, ⅜"w green grosgrain ribbon, spray adhesive, paper-backed fusible web, fabric glue and a paper motif to decorate book (cut our nutcracker motif from a pape garland).

1. Open songbook and lay it flat, cov side up. Cut a piece from red paper slightly larger than open book. Use spray adhesive to apply paper to cov of book. Trim paper even with edge cover. Close book.
2. Cut a piece from plaid fabric same size as front cover of book. Follow manufacturer's instructions to fuse w to wrong side of fabric. Cut web-back fabric 2½" narrower and 3" shorter than front cover of book. Center fabr on book and fuse in place.
3. Cut 2 lengths of ½"w ribbon ½" longer than width of fabric piece; cut lengths ½" longer than length of fab piece. Mitering lengths at corners, center ribbon lengths over edges of fabric piece; use fabric glue to secure.
4. Cutting ribbon lengths 1½" longer than width and length of fabric piece, repeat Step 3 to glue ⅜"w ribbon lengths approx. ⅛" from ½"w ribbon.
5. Tie a 10" length of ⅜"w ribbon into a bow; trim ends. Use fabric glue glue bow to book. Use spray adhesive glue paper motif to book.

ORANGE BLACK BOTTOM PIE

CRUST

1½ cups all-purpose flour
½ teaspoon salt
½ cup vegetable shortening
¼ cup cold water

FILLING

¾ cup whipping cream, divided
½ cup semisweet chocolate chips
2 tablespoons butter or margarine
2 teaspoons orange extract, divided
1 cup boiling water
1 box (3 ounces) orange-flavored gelatin
1 package (8 ounces) cream cheese, softened
1 cup confectioners sugar, sifted

DECORATIVE TOPPING

2 tablespoons water
2 tablespoons granulated sugar
1½ teaspoons unflavored gelatin
½ cup whipping cream

Delightfully rich and sweet, Orange Black Bottom Pie features a layer of chocolate topped with a creamy orange filling. Sweetened whipped cream is piped around the pie for an elegant finish.

For crust, preheat oven to 350 degrees. In a medium bowl, sift together flour and salt. Using a pastry blender or 2 knives, cut in shortening until mixture resembles coarse meal. Sprinkle with water; mix until a soft dough forms. On a lightly floured surface, use a floured rolling pin to roll out dough to ⅛-inch thickness. Transfer to an ungreased 9-inch deep-dish pie pan and use a sharp knife to trim edges of dough. Prick bottom of crust with a fork. Bake 12 to 15 minutes or until light brown. Cool completely on a wire rack.

For filling, combine ¼ cup whipping cream, chocolate chips, and butter in a small saucepan. Stirring constantly, cook over low heat until smooth. Stir in 1 teaspoon orange extract. Pour into cooled crust.

Chill medium bowl and beaters from an electric mixer in refrigerator. In chilled bowl, whip remaining ½ cup whipping cream until stiff peaks form; cover and refrigerate. In another medium bowl, combine water and orange-flavored gelatin; stir until gelatin dissolves. Cool to room temperature. In a large bowl, beat cream cheese, sugar, and remaining 1 teaspoon orange extract until fluffy. Beat gelatin mixture into cream cheese mixture. Fold whipped cream into cream cheese mixture.

Pour filling evenly over chocolate mixture in crust. Cover and refrigerate until pie is set. Wash and dry medium bowl and beaters; return to refrigerator.

For decorative topping, combine water, sugar, and unflavored gelatin in a small saucepan. Cook over low heat, stirring until gelatin and sugar dissolve. Remove from heat. In chilled bowl, beat whipping cream until soft peaks form. Add sugar mixture and beat until stiff peaks form. Transfer topping to a pastry bag fitted with a large star tip. Pipe a decorative border along top edge of pie. Cover and refrigerate until ready to serve.

Yield: about 8 servings

CHRISTMAS FUN FOR KIDS

Children love the excitement of Christmas, and a classroom celebration is a great way for them to begin the holidays. These party ideas are perfect for preschool or elementary students — and they're easy on your budget, too! We have a collection of simple treats that are sure to appeal to little folks, along with adorable party favors and fun, easily supervised activities. Our "pin the nose on the snowman" game (instructions are given on page 73) is a delightful source of amusement. You may even have as much fun as the kids!

Gingerbread Cookies

Peanut Butter Snack Mix

Christmas Tree Suckers

Popcorn Wreaths

Cookie Cutter Sandwiches

Strawberry Punch

PEANUT BUTTER SNACK MIX

- 2 bags (11 ounces each) small pretzels
- 1 package (12 ounces) peanut butter-flavored chips
- 1 jar (7 ounces) marshmallow creme
- ½ cup butter or margarine
- 4 tablespoons honey
- 4 tablespoons milk
- 6 cups confectioners sugar, sifted

Place pretzels in a very large bowl. Stirring constantly, melt peanut butter chips in a medium saucepan over low heat. Add next 4 ingredients; stir until smooth. Pour peanut butter mixture over pretzels; stir until evenly coated. Coat pretzel mixture with sugar in batches. For each batch, place 2 cups sugar into a large brown paper bag. Add ⅓ pretzel mixture, close bag, and shake briefly. Spread mix on waxed paper. Cool completely. Store in an airtight container.

Yield: about 23 cups snack mix

CHRISTMAS TREE SUCKERS

- Vegetable cooking spray
- Small, round fruit-flavored decorating candies
- Lollipop sticks
- 2 cups granulated sugar
- 1 cup water
- ¾ cup light corn syrup
- 1 tablespoon butter or margarine
- ¼ teaspoon green food coloring
- ⅛ teaspoon peppermint- or spearmint-flavored oil

Spray tree-shaped lollipop mold with cooking spray. Place candies and lollipop sticks in mold; set aside.

Butter sides of a large heavy saucepan. Combine sugar, water, corn syrup, and butter in saucepan. Stirring

Perfect for party favors, these flannel snowman bags have a window to reveal the yummy Peanut Butter Snack Mix and candy tucked inside.

constantly, cook over low heat until sugar dissolves. Increase heat to medium and bring to a boil. Cover and boil 3 minutes. Stir in food coloring. Attach candy thermometer to pan, making sure thermometer does not touch bottom of pan. Continue to cook uncovered, without stirring, until syrup reaches hard crack stage (approximately 300 to 310 degrees). Test about ½ teaspoon syrup in ice water. Syrup should form brittle threads in ice water

and remain brittle when removed from the water. Remove from heat and stir i flavoring. Spoon into prepared mold i batches, keeping remaining syrup in p over low heat. As soon as syrup is firm invert mold onto aluminium foil and press on back to release suckers. Repe with remaining candies, lollipop stick and syrup. Cool suckers completely ar wrap individually with plastic wrap.

Yield: about 1½ dozen 3½-inch suckers

SNOWMAN BAGS

For each bag, you will need one
? x 13″ piece and two 4″ squares of
white flannel, a 5″ x 13″ piece of clear
lightweight vinyl (available at fabric
stores), paper-backed fusible web, white
thread, tracing paper, tissue paper, a
?″ chenille stem, orange and black
dimensional fabric paint in squeeze
bottles, polyester fiberfill, 15″ of ¼″w
white satin ribbon, 10″ of ⅞″w ribbon
for scarf, compass, pinking shears,
fabric marking pencil, seam ripper, hot
glue gun, and glue sticks.

For bag, cut a 5″ x 13″ piece from
web. Matching 1 long edge of web to 1
long edge of 7″ x 13″ flannel piece,
follow manufacturer's instructions to
fuse web to wrong side of flannel.
For window pattern, cut a 2¼″ dia.
circle from tracing paper. Draw around
pattern on center of flannel. Use pinking
shears to cut out circle.
Place flannel web side up on ironing
board. Place vinyl over web. Being
careful not to touch vinyl with iron, use
a pressing cloth and a low iron setting
fuse vinyl to flannel.
Topstitch ¼″ from edge of window.
(*Note:* Use a ¼″ seam allowance for
Steps 5 and 6. To sew vinyl, use tissue
paper on both sides of seam; tear away
tissue after sewing.) Matching right sides
and short edges, fold flannel in half.
Sew short edges together to form a tube.
Finger press seam open.
With seam at center back, finger press
tube flat. Sew raw edges together at
bottom (vinyl end) of tube.
Match each pressed line to seam at
bottom of bag; sew across each corner
1″ from point (Fig. 1).

Fig. 1

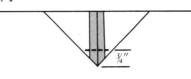

8. For casing, press top edge ½″ to
wrong side. Use a ⅜″ seam allowance
to stitch in place. Turn bag right side
out. Use seam ripper to open casing on
outside of bag at seamline. Thread
¼″w ribbon through casing.
9. For head pattern, cut a 2½″ dia.
circle from tracing paper. Use 4″ flannel
squares and pattern and follow Sewing
Shapes, page 122. Stuff head with
fiberfill. Sew final closure by hand.
10. Paint eyes and mouth black and
nose orange. Allow to dry.
11. For earmuffs, roll 5″ at each end of
chenille stem into a coil. Glue 1 coil to
each side of head. Glue head to bag.
12. For scarf, make ½″ clips in each
end of ⅞″w ribbon. Tie ribbon around
bag below head.

SNOWMAN GAME

*To play, each child receives a nose and is
blindfolded in turn to place the nose on
the snowman. The child whose nose is
closest to the proper place wins.*

You will need a 24″ x 39″ piece of
green felt, a 22″ x 29″ piece of white
felt, a 7″ square of red felt, a 6″ x 12″
piece of blue felt, a 3″ x 7″ piece of
orange felt for each nose, two 1⅛″ dia.
and five ½″ dia. black buttons with
shanks removed, three 12″ red chenille
stems, string, thumbtack, tracing paper,
transparent tape, craft glue, a 27″ long
white dowel rod with end caps, black
dimensional fabric paint in a squeeze
bottle, and Aleene's™ Tack-It™ adhesive.

1. For snowman pattern, cut a 21″
square from tracing paper (pieced as
necessary). Fold in half from top to
bottom and again from left to right. To
mark cutting line, tie 1 end of string to a
pencil. Insert thumbtack through string
10″ from pencil. Insert thumbtack in
paper as shown in Fig. 1 and mark ¼
of a circle.

Fig. 1

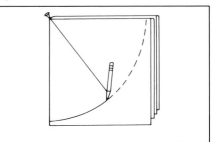

2. Repeat Step 1, cutting an 11″ square
from paper and inserting thumbtack 5″
from pencil. Cut along drawn lines;
unfold. With small circle overlapping
large circle 3½″, tape circles together.
3. (*Note:* Use craft glue for Steps 3 - 6.)
Use pattern and cut snowman from
white felt. With snowman centered and
bottom of snowman 3″ from 1 short
edge, glue snowman to green felt.
4. Trace earmuff, mitten, and nose
patterns, page 113, onto tracing paper;
cut out. Use patterns and cut earmuffs,
mittens, and noses from felt.
5. For earmuff band, refer to photo,
page 69, and glue chenille stems over
head. Glue earmuffs and mittens to
snowman. Glue buttons to snowman for
eyes and mouth. Allow to dry.
6. For hanging sleeve, press top edge of
banner 2½″ to wrong side; unfold.
Apply a line of glue ½″ from edge on
wrong side and refold. Allow to dry.
7. Insert dowel through sleeve.
8. Use paint to number noses; allow to
dry. Follow manufacturer's instructions
to apply Tack-It™ to back of each nose.

FAMILY TRADITIONS

This year, make your family's holiday dinner an especially memorable one with these easy ideas. Plan on providing the entrée, appetizer, and beverage yourself, and ask relatives to bring traditional family dishes to complete the meal. For preserving these time-honored recipes, make our personalized recipe file set as a gift for each household. To delight your guests even more, create a "family tree" featuring ornaments made from copies of family photographs. (Instructions for the tree are given on page 79.) After dinner, everyone can gather around the tree to exchange gifts and recall past celebrations. As the stories unfold, you'll want to capture the precious moments on videotape to share again and again.

Christmas Punch

Basil-Garlic Snack Wafers

Roasted Cornish Hens
with Coriander Glaze

Dressed up with purchased poultry leg frills, tender Roasted Cornish Hens with Coriander Glaze make a mouth-watering main course. Napkins tied with heart ornaments add a loving touch to the table presentation.

*A*t Christmastime, our homes take on a festive air as we adorn each room with cheerful decorations. For the busiest of rooms — the kitchen — we look for just the right trimmings to enhance the holiday mood. This collection of ornaments and accessories was designed to add an extra measure of merriment to your kitchen — or any other room! In fact, many of the ''ingredients'' you'll use to create them can be found in your own pantry and cupboards. Your family and friends will be delighted to discover the delectable decorations on display at your house this Christmas!

MERRY
ACCENTS
FROM THE
PANTRY

*B*rightening our
[wi]nter days, cardinals seem
[to] call "good cheer, good
[che]er" with their happy
[so]ng. Their brilliant
[pl]umage is another reason
[the]se little redbirds are a
[na]tural choice for holiday
[de]corating. With the versatile
[pr]ojects shown here and on
[th]e following pages, you can
[dr]ess up your kitchen with a
[flo]ck of woodland cardinals
[th]is Christmas. You'll find
[th]e cheery birds painted on a
[sto]ol, appliquéd on place
[m]ats and an apron, perched
[o]n a decorative birdhouse,
[an]d even atop a luscious
[ch]erry cake! There's also
[a s]et of purchased kitchen
[to]wels dressed up with red
[pi]ndot ruffles and deep green
[ri]bbon to coordinate with
[th]e decor.

[C]HERRY CARDINAL CAKES

*[Ca]rdinal decorations must be made
[a] day in advance.*

[RO]YAL ICING
   3 egg whites
2⅔ cups confectioners sugar, sifted
    Red, green, and black paste food
     coloring
[CA]KES
   1 jar (10 ounces) maraschino
     cherries
   1 box (18.25 ounces) yellow cake
     mix
   1 box (3 ounces) cherry-flavored
     gelatin

   4 eggs
  ⅔ cup vegetable oil
  ⅓ cup water
FROSTING
   7 cups confectioners sugar, sifted
   2 cups butter or margarine, softened
   4 tablespoons milk
   1 tablespoon vanilla extract

Trace cardinal decorations pattern, page 118, onto 2 separate sheets of tracing paper. Tape each pattern on a separate baking sheet. Cover with plastic wrap; secure edges with transparent tape. For royal icing, beat egg whites and sugar in a medium bowl until well blended. Divide icing evenly into 3 separate bowls. Tint icing red, green, and black. Cover red and green icings with a damp paper towel. Transfer black icing to a pastry bag fitted with a very small round tip. Using pattern as a guide, pipe black icing onto each sheet of plastic wrap, outlining bird, leaves, and berries. Fill in beak. (Do not pipe detail lines on birds and leaves at this time.) Allow icing to harden. Store remaining black icing in a resealable plastic bag in refrigerator. Use a small knife to spread red icing inside birds and berries and green icing inside leaves. Allow icing to harden at room temperature 24 hours or until completely dry.

For cakes, preheat oven to 350 degrees. Place cherries, including juice, in a food processor and coarsely chop. In a large bowl, mix cherry mixture and remaining ingredients until moistened. Using medium speed of an electric mixer, beat for 2 minutes. Pour batter into 2 greased and floured 8-inch square baking pans. Bake 30 to 35 minutes or until a toothpick inserted in center comes out clean. Cool in pans

10 minutes. Remove from pans and cool completely on a wire rack.

For frosting, beat all ingredients together in a large bowl until smooth. Reserving 2½ cups of frosting, frost sides and top of each cake. To decorate cakes, transfer remaining frosting to a pastry bag fitted with a large star tip. Pipe decorative border along top and bottom edges of each cake. Invert cardinal decorations onto a flat surface and carefully peel away plastic wrap. Refer to photo to place decorations on cakes. Pipe black icing on cakes for branches and detail lines on birds and leaves. Allow icing to harden. Store in an airtight container in refrigerator.

Yield: 2 cakes

RUFFLED KITCHEN TOWELS

For each towel, you will need 1 kitchen towel, fabric for ruffle, 1"w grosgrain ribbon, and thread to match ribbon and fabric.

1. For ruffle, measure 1 short edge (bottom) of towel; multiply by 2. Cut one 6"w fabric strip the determined measurement. For ruffle trim, cut a length from ribbon 1" longer than bottom edge of towel.
2. Press ends of ruffle strip ¼" to wrong side; press ¼" to wrong side again. Matching wrong sides, press strip in half lengthwise.
3. To gather ruffle, baste ⅜" and ¼" from raw edge; pull basting threads, drawing up gathers to fit bottom of towel. With raw edge of ruffle overlapping bottom edge of towel ½", sew ruffle to right side of towel.
4. Press ends of ribbon length ½" to wrong side. Center ribbon over raw edge of ruffle; baste in place. Topstitch close to edges of ribbon. Remove any visible basting threads.

Our no-sew appliqué design brightens a purchased place mat trimmed with ribbon. Napkins sewn from kitchen towels complement the table setting.

CARDINAL PLACE MATS AND NAPKINS

For each place mat, you will need a purchased fabric place mat (we used a white octagonal mat), one 7″ square of red print fabric and scraps of green fabric for appliqué, one 7″ square of white fabric for bird appliqué backing, ⅜″w green grosgrain ribbon, lightweight fusible interfacing, paper-backed fusible web, washable fabric glue, tracing paper, and black dimensional fabric paint in a squeeze bottle.

For each napkin, you will need one-half of a kitchen towel, thread to match towel, and 22″ of ⅜″w green grosgrain ribbon for tie.

1. For place mat, glue ribbon to place mat ⅛″ from all edges, mitering ribbon at corners. Allow to dry.

2. For appliqué, follow manufacturers' instructions to fuse interfacing, then web, to wrong sides of appliqué fabrics.

3. Trace bird, berry, and leaf patterns, page 118, onto tracing paper and cut out. Use patterns and cut pieces from fabrics.

4. Fuse bird to center of white fabric.

5. Centering lines of paint over raw edges of bird appliqué, paint over raw edges; paint beak and detail lines. Allow to dry. Cut out bird close to painted lines.

6. Place bird on place mat with tail extending approx. ½″ beyond edge of place mat; arrange leaves and berries below bird. Fuse leaves and berries in place; glue bird in place. Centering lines of paint over raw edges of leaf and berry appliqués, paint over raw edges; paint detail lines. Allow to dry.

7. For each napkin, press raw edge of towel half ¼″ to wrong side; press ¼″ to wrong side again and stitch in place. Fold napkin as desired. Tie ribbon into a bow around napkin; trim ribbon ends.

BIRDHOUSE

You will need 1 purchased unfinished wooden birdhouse, mesquite wood chips, a sprig of artificial leaves and berries, 2 artificial cardinals, dk green acrylic paint, foam brush, hot glue gun, and glue sticks.

1. Leaving roof unpainted, paint birdhouse dk green; allow to dry.

2. Glue mesquite chips to roof of house.

3. Glue birds and berry sprig to house.

Wood chip shingles and a coat of paint make this decorative birdhouse the perfect nesting place for a pair of felike cardinals.

WOODLAND GNOME TREE

*Sporting bright red
[ca]ps, the gnomes on this
[tab]letop tree are spicy
[or]ange-gingerbread cookies.
[Be]cause gnomes enjoy the
[co]mpany of their woodland
[fri]ends, we perched a flock
[of] redbirds among the
[br]anches of the tree and atop
[de]corated birdhouses. The
[Po]pcorn Icicles are created
[by] pouring a mixture of
[cor]n syrup and sugar over
[str]ings of fluffy popcorn.
[A] purchased wooden bead
[ga]rland adds a colorful
[fin]ishing touch.*

[PO]PCORN ICICLES

[Yo]u will need a sewing needle,
[twen]ty-eight 8-inch lengths of white
[thr]ead, clear acrylic spray (if icicles are
[no]t to be eaten), and the following
[ing]redients:

3 cups popped popcorn
2 cups granulated sugar
1 cup light corn syrup
½ cup water

Using needle and two lengths of
[thr]ead, knot ends of thread and string a
[8-i]nch string of popcorn. Tie a ½-inch
[loo]p at top of thread. Repeat for
[rem]aining thread lengths and popcorn.
Butter sides of a 3-quart heavy
[sau]cepan. Combine sugar, corn syrup,
[an]d water in pan. Stirring constantly,
[co]ok over medium-low heat until sugar
[dis]solves. Using a pastry brush dipped
[in] hot water, wash down any sugar
[cry]stals on sides of pan. Increase heat to

medium and bring to a boil. Do not stir
while syrup is boiling. Using a candy
thermometer, cook until syrup reaches
soft crack stage (approximately 270 to
290 degrees). Remove from heat.

Holding top of string, dip each
popcorn string in syrup, spooning syrup
over popcorn until well coated. Hang
candy-coated popcorn strings over
aluminum foil, making sure popcorn
strings do not touch. Cool completely. If
desired, spray with acrylic spray to
reduce stickiness; allow to dry. Wrap
individually in plastic wrap until ready
to decorate tree.

Yield: 2 dozen popcorn icicles

ORANGE-GINGERBREAD GNOMES

⅓ cup vegetable shortening
⅓ cup firmly packed brown sugar
1 egg
⅔ cup honey
1 teaspoon orange extract
1 teaspoon dried grated orange peel
2¾ cups all-purpose flour
1 teaspoon ground cinnamon
1 teaspoon baking soda
½ teaspoon salt
½ teaspoon ground allspice
¼ teaspoon ground ginger
2 teaspoons water
1 teaspoon red paste food coloring
Purchased white decorating icing
Black paste food coloring
Red candy-coated chocolate pieces

Preheat oven to 350 degrees. In a
large bowl, cream shortening and sugar
until fluffy. Add egg, honey, orange
extract, and orange peel; beat until
smooth. In a medium bowl, sift together
next 6 ingredients. Add dry ingredients
to creamed mixture; knead in bowl until
a soft dough forms. Trace gnome cookie

pattern, page 119, onto tracing paper;
cut out. On a lightly floured surface,
use a floured rolling pin to roll out
dough to ¼-inch thickness. Place
pattern on dough and use a sharp knife
to cut out cookies. Transfer to a greased
baking sheet. Use a drinking straw to
make a hole at the top of each cookie.
Bake 8 to 10 minutes or until edges
begin to brown. Transfer to a wire rack
to cool completely.

To decorate cookies, mix water and
red food coloring in a small bowl. Brush
mixture on cookies for stocking caps.
Transfer icing to a small bowl; tint
black. Transfer black icing to a pastry
bag fitted with a very small round tip.
Pipe icing on cookies for eyes. Use icing
to secure chocolate pieces on cookies
for noses. Allow icing to harden. Store
in an airtight container until ready to
decorate tree. Use lengths of jute to
hang cookies on tree.

Yield: about 2 dozen cookies

BIRDHOUSE ORNAMENTS

For each ornament, you will need an
unfinished wooden birdhouse ornament
(ours measures 5¼"h; available at
craft stores), a fabric piece to cover base
of ornament, twigs to cover roof of
ornament, Design Master® glossy wood
tone spray, hot glue gun, and glue
sticks.

1. Spray birdhouse ornament lightly
with wood tone spray; allow to dry.
2. Remove base from ornament. Remove
any nails from base.
3. Trimming fabric to fit and pressing
raw edges to wrong side, wrap base
with fabric; glue to secure.
4. Glue base to bottom of ornament.
5. Glue twigs to roof of ornament,
trimming to fit if necessary.

12. Place remaining pieces on greased baking sheets. Bake 10 to 15 minutes or until edges are firm. Transfer to a wire rack to cool completely.

13. To tint confectioners icing, spoon about 4 tablespoons icing into each of 6 small bowls. Use food coloring to tint icing blue, light brown, brown, red, green, and purple. Cover bowls until ready to use.

14. Using confectioners icing, ice the following pieces:

    Mary's robe - blue
    Joseph's robe - light brown
    Joseph's cloak - brown
    Kings' robes - red, green, or purple
    Donkey - brown

Transfer pieces to wire rack with waxed paper underneath and allow icing to harden.

15. Use paintbrush to apply petal dust to crowns and gifts on kings and to star.

16. To tint royal icing, spoon about ½ cup icing into a small bowl. Use food coloring to tint icing dark brown. Place dark brown and remaining white icing into separate pastry bags.

17. To assemble manger, use large round tip to pipe white royal icing along one long edge of one 1½″ x 3″

side piece. Press one long edge of remaining side piece into icing to form a ''V'' that is 2″w across top. Hold pieces in place until icing sets. Pipe icing along bottom of manger. Center manger on one 2″ x 3″ base. Hold manger in place until icing sets.

18. To assemble stable, use large round tip to pipe white royal icing along top edges of stable back. Press 1 long edge of each 2″ x 6½″ roof piece into icing. Hold in place until icing sets. Pipe icing between roof pieces at center of roof. Pipe icing along each side edge of stable back. Press 1 edge of each 5″ square side piece into icing. Hold in place until icing sets.

19. (*Note:* For Steps 19 - 23, use royal icing and indicated decorating tips to decorate pieces, allowing icing to harden.) Use dark brown icing and very small round tip to pipe Mary's hair, Joseph's beard, and braid on Joseph's headdress.

20. Use dark brown icing and small round tip to outline Joseph's clothes and bridle on donkey.

21. Use dark brown icing and grass tip to pipe mane and tail on donkey and hay in manger. Place Baby Jesus on hay before icing hardens.

STABLE BACK

22. Use white icing and small round tip to outline Mary's robe and pipe blanket on Baby Jesus.

23. Use white icing and small star tip to pipe crown trims, collars, and cuffs on kings. Use dragées to decorate crowns and collars before icing hardens.

24. To attach each king to base, use medium star tip to pipe white royal icing around bottom of king. Center king on one 2″ x 3″ base; hold in place until icing sets. Use large round tip and white royal icing to attach Mary to base. Use large round tip and dark brown royal icing to attach Joseph and donkey to bases. Allow icing to harden.

25. Arrange figures and stable. Decorate with raffia.

"STAINED GLASS" DECORATIONS

A snow-flocked tree the perfect backdrop for ese bright and colorful tained glass" decorations. e tree and star ornaments e created with salt dough d hard candies, and the ndy wreaths are shaped in iniature Bundt® cake ns. Purchased glass balls d a multicolor bead rland complement the ndy ornaments.

STAINED GLASS" RNAMENTS

te: These ornaments are for corative use only and should not be ten.

u will need tracing paper, aluminum l, pastry bag, large round (#7) corating tip, 18-gauge wire for ngers, wire cutters, clear acrylic ray, and the following ingredients:

 Vegetable cooking spray
1 cup all-purpose flour
½ cup plus 2 teaspoons water
½ cup salt
½ cup each of 5 different colors of finely crushed hard candies (about 20 candies of each color)

Trace star and tree patterns, ge 121, onto tracing paper. Place tterns on aluminum foil-lined baking eets and draw over patterns to nsfer patterns to foil. Spray foil with oking spray.

Preheat oven to 325 degrees. In a medium bowl, mix flour, water, and salt until a soft dough forms. Transfer dough to pastry bag fitted with tip. Following outlines of patterns, pipe dough onto foil. For hanger, place a small loop of wire into dough at top of each ornament. Bake 15 minutes. Cool on pans. Spoon crushed candies into sections of ornaments, filling each to top of dough. Bake 8 to 10 minutes or until candies melt. Cool 3 to 5 minutes or until ornaments are cool enough to touch. While still warm, invert ornaments onto a flat surface and carefully peel away foil. Cool completely. Spray front and back with acrylic spray; allow to dry.

Yield: about 1½ dozen 4-inch ornaments

"STAINED GLASS" WREATHS

You will need hard candies of various colors, clear acrylic spray (if wreaths are not to be eaten), plastic wrap, miniature Bundt® pan, and decorative cord for hangers.

Preheat oven to 350 degrees. Place 6 to 7 pieces of candy in bottom of each tin of a well-greased miniature Bundt® pan. Bake 7 minutes or until candies melt. Cool in pan 4 to 5 minutes. While candy is still warm and pliable, use a sharp knife to loosen edges and carefully lift out candy. (If candy becomes too cool to remove from pan, place back in heated oven for a few minutes.) If desired, spray with acrylic spray to reduce stickiness; allow to dry. Wrap individually in plastic wrap until ready to use. For hanger, tie a length of cord around each wreath.

MERRY KITCHEN ACCENTS

Holiday hospitality is always at its greatest in the family kitchen. Your friends and relatives will find the atmosphere even more inviting this year when they see these cheerful Christmas decorations. Designed with this homey room in mind, the Yuletide accents shown here and on the following pages are crafted from simple and inexpensive materials. Everyday items such as rolling pins, wooden thread spools, dustpans, and washboards are transformed into delightful decorations with a few artful touches. With wreaths for the door and arrangements for the windowsill, this collection will make your kitchen as merry as Santa's!

Covered with cheery trimmings and a darling teddy bear, a coppery dustpan becomes a festive decoration for the kitchen door or window.

Freshly laundered at the North Pole Washateria, Santa's suit is ready for his Christmas Eve deliveries. The ndowsill over your kitchen sink is the ideal location for this whimsical display.

*M*iniature rolling pins are easily transformed into cute little Santas with no-bake sculpting clay. Teamed with old-fashioned cookie cutters and a bright plaid bow, the diminutive Santas make cheerful wreath decorations. They also can be used as napkin ties when glued to red ribbons. You'll be on a roll when you start your decorating with these versatile ornaments!

ꓳꓶSTPAN DECORATION

ꓳu will need a copper-colored ꓯstpan, preserved cedar, pinecones, ꓯtificial holly with berries, 1¾" dia. ꓯss ball ornaments, 2 yds of 1⅞"w ꓯid wired ribbon, an approx. 6" high ꓯrchased teddy bear, florist wire, hot ꓯe gun, and glue sticks.

(*Note:* Refer to photo, page 96, for ꓯ steps.) Wire several stems of cedar ꓯgether. With stems over handle, glue ꓯdar to dustpan. Glue holly to dustpan ꓯer cedar.

Glue bear to dustpan over holly. Glue pinecones and ball ornaments to ꓯstpan.

Tie ribbon into a bow. Cut V-shaped ꓯtches in ribbon ends. Glue bow to ꓯstpan over handle; arrange streamers ꓯd glue in place.

ꓳRTH POLE WASHATERIA

ꓯr washboard, you will need a small ꓯshboard with flat area large enough ꓯ accommodate 6½" x 3½" sign ꓯttern (we found ours at an antique ꓯre), tracing paper, graphite transfer ꓯper, white drawing paper, red ꓯnstruction paper, black and red ꓯrmanent felt-tip pens with fine points, ꓯsign Master® glossy wood tone spray ꓯvailable at craft stores), artificial holly ꓯth berries, hot glue gun, and glue ꓯcks.

ꓯr string of clothes and basket, you ꓯl need an 18" square of red flannel, ꓯd and black thread, low-loft cotton ꓯtting, four unmatched ¼" dia. pearl ꓯttons, a ½" dia. white pom-pom, ꓯstant coffee, tracing paper, compass, ꓯric glue, cotton string, miniature ꓯthespins, a small basket, and a fabric ꓯuare to line basket.

1. (*Note:* Refer to photo, page 97, for all steps.) For sign, trace sign pattern, page 114, onto tracing paper. Use transfer paper to transfer pattern to center of white paper. Use black pen to draw over transferred lines. Use red pen to color words.

2. Cut red paper to fit flat area in washboard.

3. With design centered on paper, cut sign slightly smaller than red paper. Glue sign to center of red paper.

4. Lightly spray sign with wood tone spray. Allow to dry.

5. Glue sign and holly to washboard.

6. For clothes, dissolve 2 tablespoons instant coffee in 2 cups hot water; allow to cool. Soak flannel in coffee for several minutes. Remove from coffee and allow to dry; press.

7. For hat pattern, use compass to draw an 8" dia. circle onto tracing paper; cut out. Fold circle into quarters; unfold circle. Cut 1 quarter from circle. Discard remainder of circle.

8. (*Note:* Use a ¼" seam allowance for Steps 8 - 11.) For hat, use pattern and cut 1 hat from flannel. Matching right sides and straight edges, fold hat piece in half. Sew straight edges together. Clip seam allowance at point. Turn right side out.

9. For coat, pocket, and pants patterns, page 114, follow Tracing Patterns, page 122.

10. For coat, cut an 11" x 14" piece from flannel. Matching right sides and short edges, fold flannel piece in half. Placing coat pattern on fabric as indicated on pattern, cut out coat. Do not unfold. Leaving openings at sleeves and bottom, sew side seams of coat. Clip seam allowance at corners; turn right side out. For opening in center front of coat, cut coat open from bottom edge to neck edge.

11. For pants, use pattern and cut 2 pants pieces from flannel. Matching right sides and notches of pants pieces, sew center seams (Fig. 1a). Matching right sides and center seams, sew leg seams (Fig. 1b). Turn right side out.

Fig. 1a

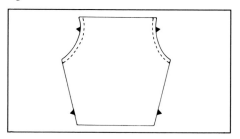

Fig. 1b

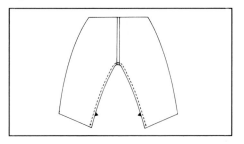

12. Press top edge of pants ⅜" to wrong side and stitch in place.

13. For fur trim, cut ½" strips from batting. Trimming strips to fit, glue batting around bottom edge of hat; along left edge of front opening of coat; around bottom edge, neck edge, and sleeves of coat; and around bottom edges of pants legs. Allow to dry.

14. Using black thread, sew buttons to coat.

15. For pockets on coat, use pattern and cut 2 pockets from flannel. Position pockets on coat; pin in place. Stitching close to side and bottom edges of pockets, sew pockets to coat.

16. Glue pom-pom to point of hat.

17. Use clothespins to hang clothes from string. Line basket with fabric square. Place clothespins in and on basket.

Wooden thread spools painted to resemble apple cores make appealing decorations. Whether lined up on a windowsill or hanging from a tiny tree in the breakfast nook, these ornaments are perfect accents for your kitchen.

OLLING PIN SANTA
REATH AND NAPKIN TIES

r each Santa, you will need a 7" long
ling pin and Design Master® glossy
od tone spray (available at craft
res), natural Maché Clay no-bake
lpting compound, red acrylic paint,
ntbrush, two 3mm black half-round
ds, tracing paper, waxed paper,
thpick, and craft glue.

r wreath, you will also need an
ificial greenery wreath, metal cookie
ters (we found ours at an antique
re), 5½"w paper ribbon, hot glue
n, and glue sticks.

r each napkin tie, you will also need
4" length of ⅞"w red satin ribbon,
t glue gun, and glue sticks.

Trace mustache, eyebrow, and beard
tterns, page 113, onto tracing paper;
t out.

(Note: Follow Steps 2 - 7 for each
nta. Refer to photos, page 98, for
ps 2 - 9.) For hat, paint 1 handle of
ling pin red; allow to dry.

Working on waxed paper, pat Maché
ay into a ⅛" to ¼" thick layer.
ce patterns on clay; draw around
tterns with a pencil. Using scissors,
t 1 mustache, 2 eyebrows, and 1
ard from clay.

Press beard and eyebrows onto
ling pin. Overlapping mustache over
ard, press mustache onto rolling pin.
r nose, form a ⅛" dia. ball of clay;
tten ball slightly and press onto
ustache. Cut a ¼" x 3" strip of clay
hat trim. Wrap strip around top edge
rolling pin, joining ends at back.
Use toothpick to press lines into clay
resemble fur and hair. Allow clay to
 overnight.

6. Carefully remove clay pieces from
rolling pin. Glue pieces back in place to
secure. Glue half-round beads to Santa
for eyes. Allow to dry.

7. Spray Santa lightly with wood tone
spray; allow to dry.

8. For wreath, tie ribbon into a bow.
Cut V-shaped notches in ribbon ends.
Hot glue bow, Santas, and cookie
cutters to wreath.

9. For each napkin tie, hot glue Santa to
center of ribbon length.

MINI APPLE CHRISTMAS TREE

You will need a miniature artificial
Christmas tree (ours measures 16" tall),
miniature baskets, cinnamon sticks,
1¼" dia. unfinished wooden apples,
1⅛" high wooden spools, red and
cream spray paint, Design Master®
glossy wood tone spray (available at
craft stores), glossy clear acrylic spray,
red and brown acrylic paint, small
paintbrushes, small preserved leaves,
anise stars, natural-colored raffia, nylon
line, hot glue gun, glue sticks, and a
kitchen towel.

1. (*Note:* Allow paint and acrylic spray
to dry between coats.) For each whole
apple ornament, spray paint apple red.
Spray apple lightly with wood tone
spray. Spray apple with clear acrylic
spray.

2. For each apple core ornament, spray
paint spool cream. Use acrylic paint to
paint top and bottom of spool red to
resemble an apple core. Use brown paint
to paint seeds on spool.

3. For hanger for each whole apple or
apple core ornament, knot ends of a 4"
length of nylon line together; glue knot
to top of apple. For stem, glue a small
piece of cinnamon stick to top of each
apple.

4. Glue 1 leaf to stem of each apple core
ornament.

5. For hanger for each anise star
ornament, knot ends of a 4" length of
raffia together; glue knot to back of star.

6. For each basket ornament, fill basket
with cinnamon sticks.

7. To decorate tree, hang ornaments on
tree. Tie raffia into a bow. Place bow at
top of tree; arrange streamers among
branches. For tree skirt, drape towel
around base of tree.

*T*hese decorative
topiaries are easy to create
by coating plastic foam
shapes with split peas and
a variety of dried herbs.
Cinnamon sticks make
wonderfully realistic
"trunks," and whole anise
stars, ribbon, pasta bows,
and other accents embellish
each tree. For display, plain
terra-cotta flowerpots can
be dressed up using a simple
sponge-painting technique,
more dried materials, and
ribbon. A bouquet of grain
tied with pretty wired ribbon
makes an attractive accent.

TOPIARY TREES

For each tree, you will need a plastic
foam shape (we used 2", 3", and
4" dia. balls and a 7" high cone),
desired dried material(s) to cover shape
(we used chives, rosemary, oregano,
split peas, and bay leaves), a gallon-size
resealable plastic bag, thick craft glue,
foam brush, hot glue gun and glue sticks
(optional), 1 or 2 cinnamon sticks for
trunk, a terra-cotta flowerpot (we used
2⅝", 3⅜", and 4¼" high pots),
floral foam to fill pot to ½" from rim,
sheet moss, desired dried material(s) to
use with sheet moss to cover floral foam
(optional; we used chives, rosemary,
and red beans), small pieces of cellulose
sponge, desired colors of acrylic paint
(we used burgundy, lt blue green, blue
green, grey, and metallic gold), raffia or
⅜"w grosgrain ribbon (optional), and
desired items to decorate tree (we used
anise stars, bay leaves, a length of
leather lacing tied into a bow, a piece of
bow tie pasta painted with green food
coloring, a dried cranberry, and
1½"w wired ribbon).

1. To paint flowerpot, dampen sponge
pieces and squeeze out excess water.
Use sponge pieces and a stamping
motion to lightly paint pot, rim of pot,
or top edge of rim with desired colors of
paint. Allow to dry.
2. If desired, tie raffia into a bow and
glue to pot or glue grosgrain ribbon
around rim of pot.
3. Place floral foam in pot.
4. (*Note:* For bay leaf tree, follow Step 4
to cover foam ball with bay leaves. For
all other trees, follow Step 5 to cover
foam shape with other dried materials.)
Use a pencil to mark a dot on ball for
bottom. Leaving a dime-size area
uncovered at bottom of ball and slightly

overlapping side edges of leaves, glue a
ring of leaves around dot. Overlapping
second ring over first ring, glue a
second ring of leaves around ball. Using
smaller leaves for top area of ball,
repeat until entire ball is covered.
5. Place desired dried material(s) into
plastic bag. Use foam brush to apply
craft glue to foam shape. Place shape
in bag and shake bag until shape is
covered with dried material(s). Remove
shape from bag and allow to dry.
6. For trunk, insert 1 or 2 cinnamon
sticks 1" into foam shape. Insert
cinnamon stick trunk at least 1" into
floral foam in pot.
7. Cover floral foam with sheet moss. If
desired, place chives, rosemary, or red
beans on top of sheet moss.
8. To decorate tree, tie ribbon around
trunk or glue desired items to tree.

GRAIN BOUQUET

You will need dried rye, dried sweet
Annie, florist wire, wire cutters, and
desired wired ribbons.

1. Arrange rye and sweet Annie together
in a bundle; wrap bundle with wire to
secure.
2. Tie ribbons into bows around bundle;
trim ends. Arrange bows and streamers
as desired.

Suspended from an extra-long cinnamon stick, this appliquéd wall hanging features a tin punch star and lively gingerbread boys who look as if they've just jumped from the pages of a children's book.

GINGERBREAD BOY PILLOWS AND WALL HANGING

Note: Supplies list is written for 1 pillow with amounts for wall hanging in parentheses.

For each pillow or wall hanging, you will need one (two) 8″ x 10″ piece(s) of brown wool fabric, one (three) 8″ x 10″ piece(s) of fabric for background, two (six) 1⅞″ x 10″ strips and two (four) 1⅞″ x 8″ strips of fabric for inner border, four (eight) 1⅞″ squares of fabric for border block, two 1⅞″ x 12¾″ (1½″ x 34½″) strips and two 1⅞″ x 13½″ (1½″ x 12¾″) strips of fabric for outer border, one 13½″ x 15½″ (15″ x 38″) piece of fabric for backing, thread to coordinate with fabrics, dk brown and black embroidery floss, two (four) ½″ dia. black buttons for buttons on gingerbread boy(s), four (eight) ⅝″ dia. buttons for border blocks, polyester fiberfill, tracing paper and fabric glue.

For wall hanging, you will also need a 9″ square of red wool fabric, a 2″w and 2¾ yd long bias strip of fabric (pieced as necessary), low-loft polyester bonded batting, 1 medium Tin Punch Star Ornament (page 108), one 17″ long cinnamon stick, and two 2½″ lengths of ⅝″w grosgrain ribbon for hanging loops.

PILLOW

1. Trace gingerbread boy pattern, page 117, onto tracing paper and cut out.

2. (*Note:* Refer to photo, page 104, for remaining steps.) For appliqué, use pattern and cut 1 gingerbread boy from brown wool. On wrong side of appliqué, apply a line of glue close to edge. Center appliqué, glue side down

right side of background fabric; press
o place. Allow to dry.
Using 3 strands of dk brown floss,
ork Blanket Stitch, page 123, along
ge of appliqué.
Cutting through background fabric
ly, cut a 2″ slit in fabric behind
gerbread boy. Stuff lightly with
erfill; whipstitch opening closed.
For eyes, use 12 strands of black floss
d work Colonial Knots, page 123. For
ttons, sew black buttons to appliqué.
(Note: For Steps 6 - 9, match raw
ges and pin fabric pieces right sides
gether. Use a ¼″ seam allowance.
ess seam allowances to 1 side unless
nerwise indicated.) For inner borders,
w 10″ long strips to side edges of
ckground. Sew 1⅞″ squares to short
ges of 8″ long strips. Sew strips with
ached border blocks to top and
ttom edges of background.
Sew ⅝″ dia. buttons to border
ocks.
For outer borders, sew 12¾″ long
ips to side edges of inner border. Sew
½″ long strips to top and bottom
ges of inner border.
Place pillow front and backing
gether. Leaving an opening for
rning, sew front and backing together.
ip corners diagonally; turn right side
t and press. Stuff pillow with fiberfill.
w final closure by hand.

ALL HANGING
Follow Steps 1 - 7 of Pillow
structions to make 2 gingerbread boy
ocks.
For star pattern, draw around Tin
nch Star Ornament on tracing paper.
tting ½″ outside drawn line, cut out
ttern. Use star pattern, red wool, and
maining background fabric piece and
llow Steps 2 and 3 of Pillow
structions.

Dressed up with a red bow and a fruity "flower," this raffia tree topper is a larger version of the braided tree decorations. The "cranberries" on the dried fruit slice are actually red wooden beads.

3. (*Note:* For Steps 3 and 4, match raw
edges and pin fabric pieces right sides
together. Use a ¼″ seam allowance.
Press seam allowances to 1 side unless
otherwise indicated.) Sew remaining
10″ long strips to side edges of star
appliqué background. Sew gingerbread
boy blocks to top and bottom edges of
star appliqué background.
4. For outer borders, sew 34½″ long
strips to side edges of inner border. Sew
12¾″ long strips to top and bottom
edges of inner border.
5. Cut 2 pieces of batting same size as
backing fabric. Place backing fabric
wrong side up on a flat surface.
Matching edges, place both layers of
batting on backing fabric. Center front of
wall hanging, right side up, on batting.
Stitching from corner to corner and side
to side, hand baste all layers together.
6. To quilt wall hanging, machine stitch
along seams around inner borders and
border blocks.

7. Trim batting and backing even with
front of wall hanging.
8. For binding, press 1 end of bias strip
½″ to wrong side. Matching wrong
sides, press strip in half lengthwise;
press long edges to center. Beginning
with unpressed end at center bottom of
wall hanging and mitering corners,
insert raw edge of wall hanging between
pressed edges of binding; baste binding
in place. Stitching close to inner edge of
binding, sew binding in place. Remove
any visible basting threads.
9. Center Tin Punch Star Ornament on
red star and glue in place. Allow to dry.
10. For hanging loops, fold each length
of ribbon in half to form a loop. With
loops 2″ from each side of wall
hanging, hand sew ends of each loop to
back of wall hanging, leaving approx. 1″
of each loop exposed at top of wall
hanging. Insert cinnamon stick through
loops.

GINGERBREAD TREE

Smells and tastes from the kitchen fill the branches of this spicy seven-foot-tall tree, evoking memories of long ago Christmases.

Two "recipes" make the sweet garlands that wind around the branches of the tree. On one garland, we combined unshelled peanuts, ⅜" dia. red wooden beads, and Dried Fruit Slices (this page). On the other garland, cinnamon sticks, red wooden beads, and fabric yo-yos (Step 9, Tree Skirt instructions, page 111) are strung together. A large needle was used to thread the "ingredients" onto heavy thread.

Handmade from simple things, a variety of ornaments adorns the tree. Gingerbread Boys (page 110), dusted with flour and fresh from the oven, tempt the senses. Three sizes of Tin Punch Star Ornaments (this page) sparkle and shine. Braided Raffia Ornaments are miniature versions of the Braided Raffia Tree Topper (both on this page).

For the grapefruit slice ornaments, we tied a knot at the center of several 13" lengths of red raffia, hot glued the knot to the top of a dried grapefruit slice, and then knotted the ends of the raffia together to form a hanger. Fabric-lined baskets filled with peanuts are trimmed with red raffia bows and small Tin Punch Star Ornaments. Tea infusers are a charming substitute for shiny ball ornaments.

Made from fabrics with an old-fashioned look, a pieced Tree Skirt (page 111) wraps the trunk of our tree.

These things bring back to our senses the pleasure of an evening in a Christmas kitchen.

TIN PUNCH STAR ORNAMENTS

You will need aluminum flashing (available at hardware stores); tracing paper; utility scissors; awl or ice pick; hammer; scrap piece of soft wood; and hot glue gun, glue sticks, and nylon line for hangers (optional).

1. (*Note:* Follow Steps 1 - 3 for each ornament.) Use desired star pattern, page 116, and follow Tracing Patterns, page 122. Place pattern on flashing and use a pencil to draw around pattern; use scissors to cut out star.
2. Place star on wood. Place pattern on star. Use awl and hammer to punch holes where indicated by dots on pattern.
3. If desired, cut an 8" length of nylon line for hanger; knot ends together. Glue knot to top back of star.

DRIED FRUIT SLICES

You will need apples, oranges, and grapefruits; wire cake racks; paring knife; lemon juice; salt; paper towels; and matte clear acrylic spray.

1. Cut each fruit crosswise into ¼" thick slices; discard end pieces.
2. For apple slices, soak slices for 20 minutes in a mixture of 2 cups lemon juice and 3 tablespoons salt. Remove slices from mixture and blot with paper towels to remove excess moisture.
3. For apple, orange, and grapefruit slices, place slices on cake racks. Dry in oven at 150 degrees for approx. 6 hours; turn slices over if edges begin to curl. When dried, slices should be pliable and have a leathery feel.
4. Spray each side of slices with 2 coats of acrylic spray, allowing to dry between coats.

BRAIDED RAFFIA ORNAMENT AND TREE TOPPER

Note: Instructions are written for one ornament with amounts for tree topper in parentheses.

You will need one 18" (36") long ½" (1½") thick bundle of natural-colored raffia, 10" (20") of 20-gauge florist wire, and one (seven) ⅜" dia. red wooden bead(s).

For each ornament, you will also need 1 dried apple or orange slice (Dried Fruit Slices, this page), 8" of 2-ply jute, and a large needle.

For tree topper, you will also need one ¼" thick bundle of red raffia in 30" - 36" lengths, 1 dried grapefruit slice (Dried Fruit Slices, this page), hot glue gun, and glue sticks.

1. (*Note:* Refer to photos, pages 107 and 109, for all steps.) For braid, wrap 2" (5") of 1 end of wire around natural-colored raffia bundle 3" (5") from 1 end. Braid raffia 9" (20") toward remaining end. Cross ends of braid to form a loop; wrap remaining wire around both ends of braid to secure. Trim ends of raffia even.
2. For each ornament, use needle to thread jute through center of fruit slice, through bead, and back through fruit slice. Place fruit slice, bead side up, over wire on braided raffia. Knot ends of jute around raffia; trim ends close to knot.
3. For tree topper, tie red raffia into a bow. Glue bow to braid over wire. Glue grapefruit slice to center of bow. Glue beads to center of grapefruit slice.

Good things from the kitchen abound on this cozy tree! Lovable gingerbread boys are complemented by tin punch *ars, dried fruit slices, braided raffia ornaments, fabric-lined baskets of peanuts, and purchased tea infusers. Two* *arlands feature peanuts, dried fruit slices, cinnamon sticks, red wooden beads, and flower-like fabric yo-yos.*

PATTERNS

TABLE RUNNER
AND COCKTAIL NAPKINS

(Page 66)

POINSETTIA SALAD BOWL

(Page 53)

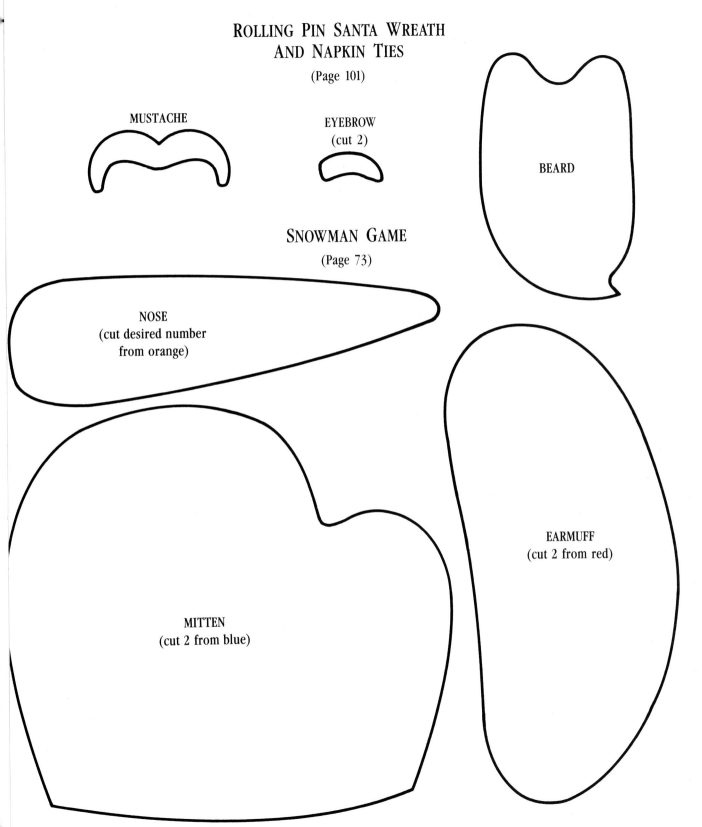

ROLLING PIN SANTA WREATH AND NAPKIN TIES

(Page 101)

MUSTACHE

EYEBROW
(cut 2)

BEARD

SNOWMAN GAME

(Page 73)

NOSE
(cut desired number
from orange)

EARMUFF
(cut 2 from red)

MITTEN
(cut 2 from blue)

PATTERNS (continued)

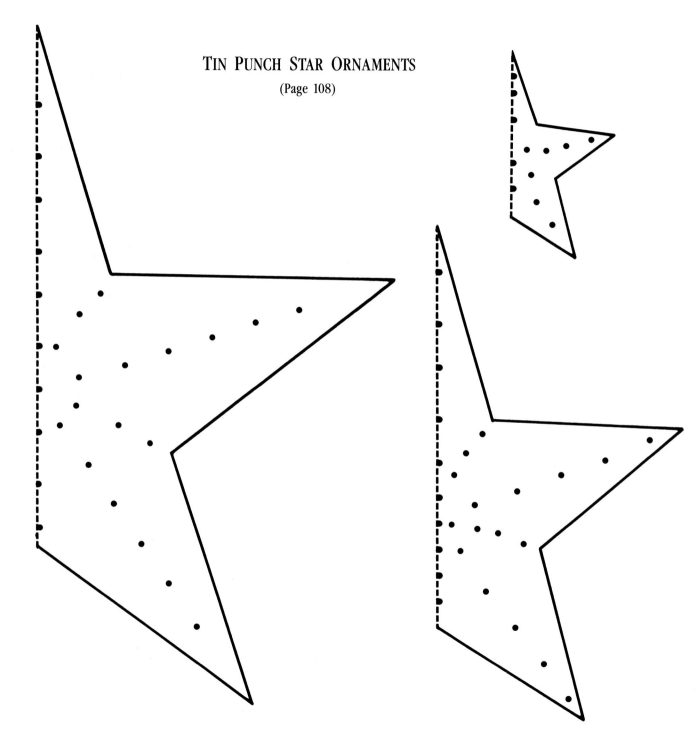

TIN PUNCH STAR ORNAMENTS
(Page 108)

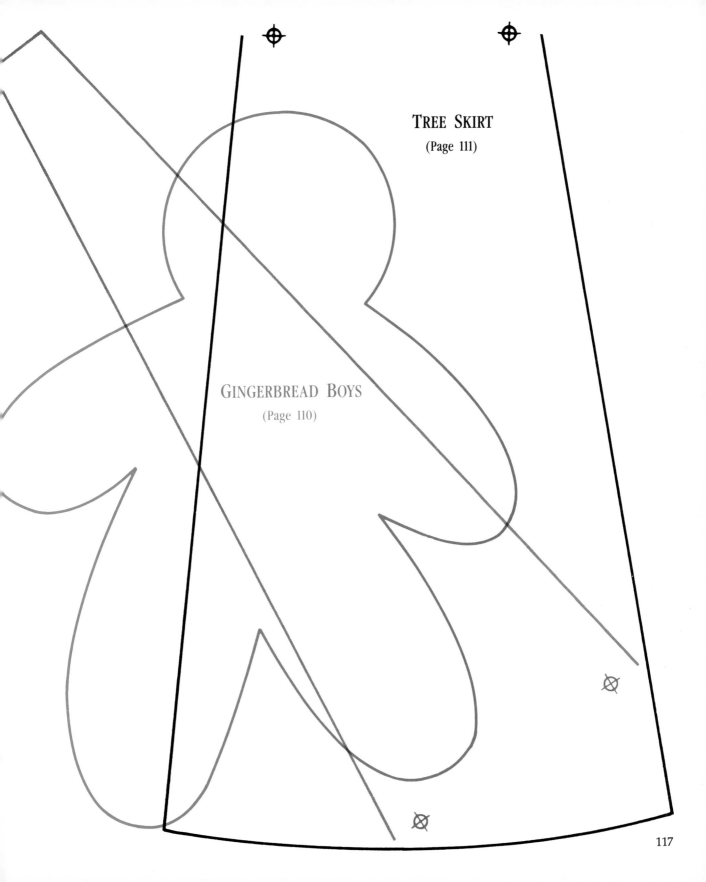

TREE SKIRT
(Page 111)

GINGERBREAD BOYS
(Page 110)

117

PATTERNS (continued)

TEAPOT COOKIES
(Page 56)

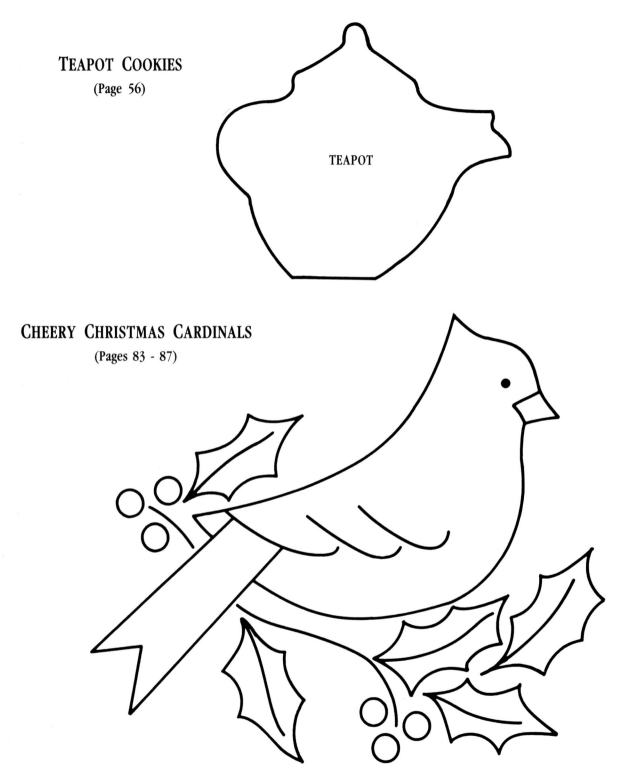

TEAPOT

CHEERY CHRISTMAS CARDINALS
(Pages 83 - 87)

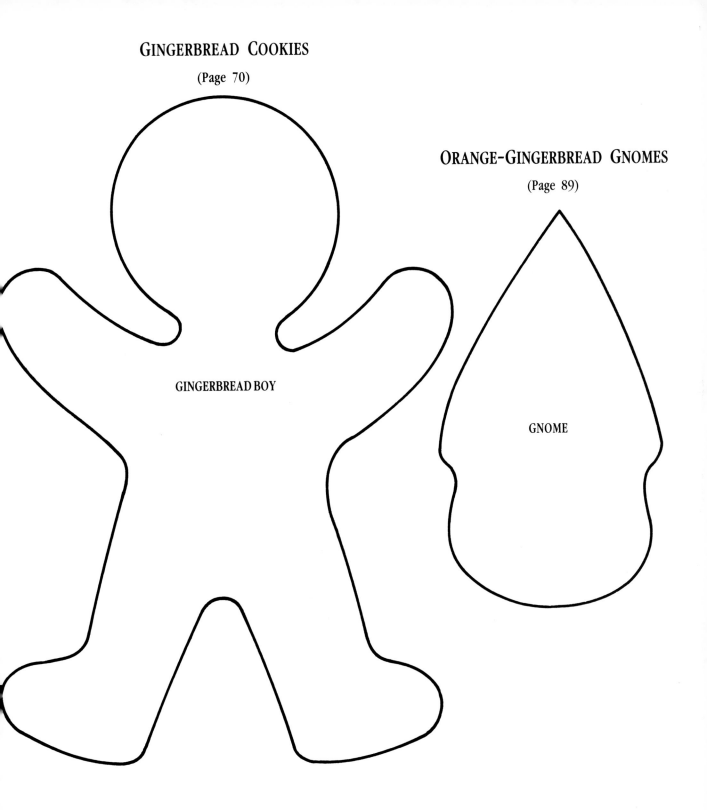

GINGERBREAD COOKIES

(Page 70)

ORANGE-GINGERBREAD GNOMES

(Page 89)

GINGERBREAD BOY

GNOME

PATTERNS (continued)

GINGERBREAD NATIVITY

(Pages 91 - 92)

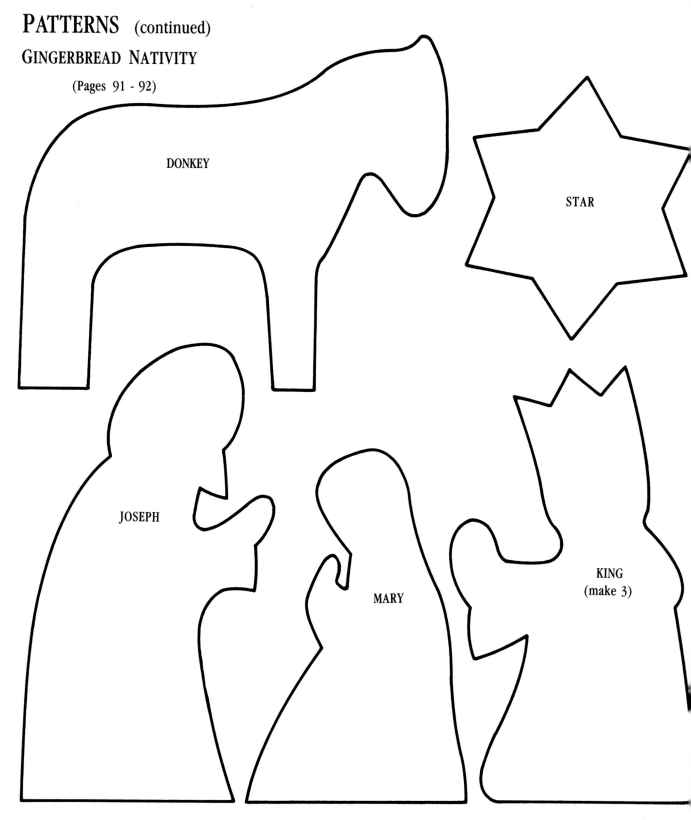

DONKEY

STAR

JOSEPH

MARY

KING
(make 3)

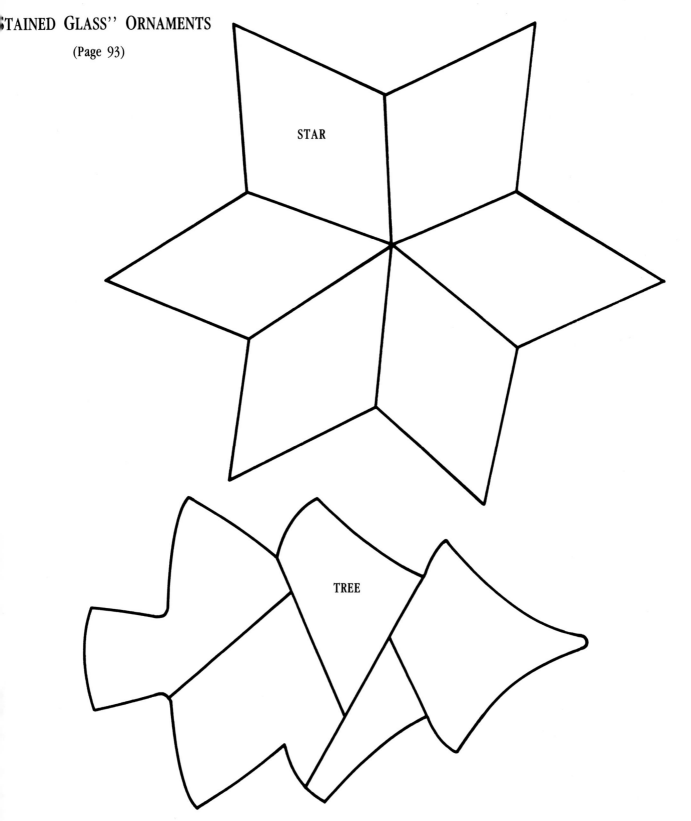

STAR

TREE

GENERAL INSTRUCTIONS

TRACING PATTERNS

When one-half of pattern (indicated by dashed line on pattern) is shown, fold tracing paper in half and place fold along dashed line of pattern. Trace pattern half, marking all placement symbols and markings; turn folded paper over and draw over all markings. Unfold pattern and lay flat. Cut out pattern.

When entire pattern is shown, place tracing paper over pattern and trace pattern, marking all placement symbols and markings. Cut out pattern.

SEWING SHAPES

1. Center pattern on wrong side of 1 fabric piece and use fabric marking pencil to draw around pattern. DO NOT CUT OUT SHAPE.
2. Place fabric pieces right sides together. Leaving an opening for turning, carefully sew pieces together directly on pencil line.
3. Leaving a ¼" seam allowance, cut out shape. Clip seam allowance at curves and corners. Turn shape right side out. Use the rounded end of a small crochet hook to completely turn small areas.

FABRIC BAG

1. To determine width of fabric needed, add ½" to finished width of bag; to determine length of fabric needed, double the finished height of bag and add 1½". Cut fabric the determined width and length.
2. With right sides together and matching short edges, fold fabric in half; finger press folded edge (bottom of bag). Using a ¼" seam allowance

and thread to match fabric, sew sides of bag together.
3. Press top edge of bag ¼" to wrong side; press ½" to wrong side again and stitch in place.
4. For bag with a flat bottom, match each side seam to fold line at bottom of bag; sew across each corner 1" from point (Fig. 1). Turn bag right side out.

Fig. 1

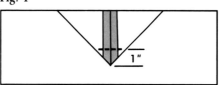

STENCILING

1. For stencil, cut a piece of acetate 1" larger on all sides than entire pattern. Center acetate over pattern and use a permanent felt-tip pen with fine point to trace pattern. Place acetate piece on cutting mat and use craft knife to cut out stencil, making sure edges are smooth.
2. (*Note:* If desired, use removable tape to mask any cutout areas on stencil next to area being painted.) Hold or tape stencil in place. Use a clean, dry stencil brush for each color of paint. Dip brush in paint and remove excess paint on a paper towel. Brush should be almost dry to produce good results. Beginning at edge of cutout area, apply paint in a stamping motion. If desired, shade design by stamping additional paint around edge of cutout area. Carefully remove stencil and allow paint to dry.

JAR LID FINISHING

1. For jar lid insert, use flat part of a jar lid (same size as jar lid used in storing food) as a pattern and cut 1 circle each from cardboard, batting, and fabric. Matching edges, glue batting to cardboard. Center fabric circle right side up on batting; glue edge of fabric to batting.
2. Just before presenting gift, remove screw ring from filled jar, being careful not to break seal of lid. Place jar lid insert in screw ring and screw in place over lid. If seal of lid is broken, jar must be refrigerated.

GIFT BOX

Note: Use this technique to cover cardboard boxes that are unassembled or are easily unfolded, such as cake or pie boxes.

1. Unfold box to be covered. Cut a piece of wrapping paper 1" larger on all sides than unfolded box. Place wrapping paper right side down on a flat surface.
2. For a small box, apply spray adhesive to outside of entire box. Place box, adhesive side down, on paper; press firmly to secure.
3. For a large box, apply spray adhesive to bottom of box. Center box, adhesive side down, on paper; press firmly to secure. Applying spray adhesive to 1 section at a time, repeat to secure remaining sections of box to paper.
4. Use a craft knife to cut paper even with edges of box. If box has slits, use craft knife to cut through slits from inside of box.
5. Reassemble box.

CROSS STITCH
COUNTED CROSS STITCH
Work 1 Cross Stitch to correspond to each colored square on the chart. For horizontal rows, work stitches in journeys (Fig. 1). For vertical rows, complete each stitch as shown in Fig. 2.

Fig. 1

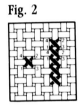

Fig. 2

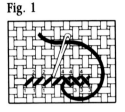

BACKSTITCH
For outline detail, Backstitch (shown on chart and color key by black or colored straight lines) should be worked after the design has been completed (Fig. 3).

Fig. 3

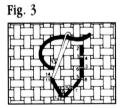

EMBROIDERY
BLANKET STITCH
Referring to Fig. 1a, come up at 1. Go down at 2 and come up at 3, keeping the thread below the point of the needle. Continue working in this manner, going down at even numbers and coming up at odd numbers (Fig. 1b).

Fig. 1a

Fig. 1b

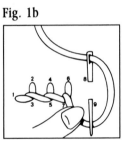

COLONIAL KNOT
Bring thread up at 1 and wrap around needle. Bring thread over needle and back under (Fig. 2) to form a figure eight. Insert needle close to 1, holding end of thread with non-stitching fingers. Tighten knot; then pull needle through fabric, holding thread until it must be released.

Fig. 2

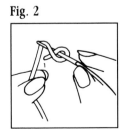

PLASTIC CANVAS
TENT STITCH
This stitch is worked over 1 intersection as shown in Fig. 1.

Fig. 1

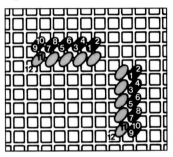

BACKSTITCH
This stitch is worked over completed stitches to outline or define (Fig. 2). It is sometimes worked over more than 1 thread.

Fig. 2

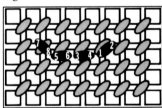

OVERCAST STITCH
This stitch covers the edge of the canvas (Fig. 3). It may be necessary to go through the same hole more than once to get an even coverage on the edge, especially at the corners.

Fig. 3

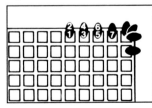

KITCHEN TIPS

MEASURING INGREDIENTS

Liquid measuring cups have a rim above the measuring line to keep liquid ingredients from spilling. Nested measuring cups are used to measure dry ingredients, butter, shortening, and peanut butter. Measuring spoons are used for measuring both dry and liquid ingredients.

To measure flour or granulated sugar: Dip nested measuring cup into ingredient and level top of cup with knife. Do not pack down with spoon.

To measure confectioners sugar: If necessary, sift sugar to remove any lumps. Spoon lightly into nested measuring cup and level top of cup with knife.

To measure brown sugar: Pack into nested measuring cup and level top of cup with knife. Sugar should hold its shape when removed from cup.

To measure dry ingredients equaling less than ¼ cup: Dip measuring spoon into ingredient and level top of spoon with knife.

To measure butter, shortening, or peanut butter: Pack firmly into nested measuring cup and level top of cup with knife.

To measure liquids: Use a liquid measuring cup placed on a flat surface. Pour ingredient into cup and check measuring line at eye level.

To measure honey or syrup: For more accurate measurement, lightly spray measuring cup or spoon with cooking spray before measuring so the liquid will release easily from cup or spoon.

TESTS FOR CANDY MAKING

There are two methods to determine the correct temperature of cooked candy. The first method is to use a candy thermometer. Before each use, check the accuracy of your candy thermometer by attaching it to the side of a small saucepan of water, making sure thermometer does not touch bottom of pan. Bring water to a boil. Thermometer should register 212 degrees when water begins to boil. If not, adjust the temperature range for each candy consistency accordingly. When using a candy thermometer, insert thermometer into candy mixture, making sure thermometer does not touch bottom of pan. Read temperature at eye level.

The second method is the cold water test. After cooking candy to desired temperature range, remove pan from heat and drop about ½ teaspoon of candy mixture into a cup of ice water. Use a fresh cup of water for each test. Use the following descriptions to determine if candy has reached the correct consistency:

Soft Ball Stage (234 to 240 degrees): candy can be rolled into a soft ball in ice water but will flatten when held in your hand.

Firm Ball Stage (242 to 248 degrees): candy can be rolled into a firm ball in ice water but will flatten if pressed when removed from the water.

Hard Ball Stage (250 to 268 degrees): candy can be rolled into a hard ball in ice water and will remain hard when removed from the water.

Soft Crack Stage (270 to 290 degrees): candy will form hard threads in ice water but will soften when removed from the water.

Hard Crack Stage (300 to 310 degrees): candy will form brittle threads in ice water and will remain brittle when removed from the water.

CANNING INSTRUCTIONS

Wash jars and bands in hot, soapy water; rinse well. Place jars on a rack a large Dutch oven. Place lids and bands in a saucepan; cover jars, lids, and bands with water. Bring water in Dutch oven to a boil; boil 10 minutes. Bring water in saucepan to a simmer (not boiling). Remove both pans from heat, leaving jars, lids, and bands in h water until ready to use. Immediately before filling, remove jars from hot water and drain well. Fill hot jars to within ¼ inch of tops. Wipe jar rims and threads. Quickly cover with lids and screw bands on tightly. For jelly, invert jars 5 minutes; turn upright to cool. For jams, butters, marmalades, and conserves, use water-bath method as directed by USDA, referring to recipe for processing time. One hour after canning, check seals. Lids should be curved down or remain so when pressed.

SOFTENING BUTTER OR MARGARINE

To soften butter, remove wrapper from butter and place on a microwave-safe plate. Microwave 1 stick 20 to 30 seconds at Medium-low (30%).

SUBSTITUTING HERBS

To substitute fresh herbs for dried, use 1 tablespoon fresh chopped herbs for ½ teaspoon dried herbs.

IIPPING CREAM
For greatest volume, chill a glass
wl, beaters, and cream until well
illed before whipping. In warm
ather, place chilled bowl over ice
ile whipping cream.

TTING COOKIE SHAPES
To cut out cookie shapes, dip cookie
tter in flour to keep dough from
cking to cutter.

**LTING CHOCOLATE OR ALMOND
RK**
To melt chocolate, place chopped or
aved chocolate in top of a double
iler (or in a heat-proof bowl over a
icepan of water) over hot, not
iling, water. Stir occasionally until
lted. Remove from heat and use for
ping as desired. If necessary,
ocolate may be returned to heat to
melt.

ASTING NUTS
To toast nuts, spread nuts evenly on
ungreased baking sheet. Stirring
quently, bake 7 to 10 minutes in a
eheated 350 degree oven.

LLING OUT PIE DOUGH
Tear off four 24-inch long pieces of
stic wrap. Overlapping long edges,
ce two pieces of wrap on a slightly
mp, flat surface; smooth out
inkles. Place dough in center of
ap. Overlapping long edges of
maining pieces of wrap, cover dough.
e rolling pin to roll out dough
nches larger than diameter of pie
ate. Remove top pieces of wrap.
vert dough into pie plate. Remove
maining pieces of wrap.

BEATING EGG WHITES
For greatest volume, beat egg whites
at room temperature in a clean, dry
metal or glass bowl.

SHREDDING CHEESE
To shred cheese easily, place
wrapped cheese in freezer for 10 to
20 minutes before shredding.

EQUIVALENT MEASUREMENTS

1 tablespoon	=	3 teaspoons
⅛ cup (1 fluid ounce)	=	2 tablespoons
¼ cup (2 fluid ounces)	=	4 tablespoons
⅓ cup	=	5⅓ tablespoons
½ cup (4 fluid ounces)	=	8 tablespoons
¾ cup (6 fluid ounces)	=	12 tablespoons
1 cup (8 fluid ounces)	=	16 tablespoons or ½ pint
2 cups (16 fluid ounces)	=	1 pint
1 quart (32 fluid ounces)	=	2 pints
½ gallon (64 fluid ounces)	=	2 quarts
1 gallon (128 fluid ounces)	=	4 quarts

HELPFUL FOOD EQUIVALENTS

½ cup butter	=	1 stick butter
1 square baking chocolate	=	1 ounce chocolate
1 cup chocolate chips	=	6 ounces chocolate chips
2¼ cups packed brown sugar	=	1 pound brown sugar
3½ cups confectioners sugar	=	1 pound confectioners sugar
2 cups granulated sugar	=	1 pound granulated sugar
4 cups all-purpose flour	=	1 pound all-purpose flour
1 cup shredded cheese	=	4 ounces cheese
3 cups sliced carrots	=	1 pound carrots
½ cup chopped celery	=	1 rib celery
½ cup chopped onion	=	1 medium onion
1 cup chopped green pepper	=	1 large green pepper

RECIPE INDEX

A

Almond Pancake Mix, 9
APPETIZERS AND SNACKS:
  Basil-Garlic Snack Wafers, 78
  Cheddar Spread, 33
  Chocolate-Mint Cheese Ball Mix, 18
  Italian Cheese Snacks, 39
  Peanut Butter Snack Mix, 72
  Sausage-Cream Cheese Squares, 65
  Sesame Seed Snack Crackers, 27
  Shrimp Spread, 64
  Sugared Cranberry Trail Mix, 29
  Turkey Nachos, 49
Apple-Cinnamon Cookies, 11

B

Basil-Garlic Snack Wafers, 78
BEVERAGES:
  Chocolate-Almond Coffee Mix, 25
  Chocolate Eggnog, 66
  Christmas Punch, 78
  Cranberry-Champagne Cocktails, 66
  Honey-of-a-Punch, 49
  Orange-Nutmeg Tea Mix, 15
  Peach Eggnog, 35
  Peach Wine Coolers, 40
  Rosemary Tea, 57
  Silver Bells Punch, 57
  Strawberry Punch, 71
Brandied Strawberries, 8
BREADS:
  Oatmeal-Rye Rolls, 49
  Orange-Pecan Bread, 31
  Snowman Bread, 22
Buttermilk Fudge, 37
Buttermilk Pecan Pies, 56

C

CAKES:
  Cherry Cardinal Cakes, 83
  Glazed Lemon Cheesecake, 52
  Pumpkin Cheesecake Squares, 61
  Sugar-and-Spice Pound Cake, 14
CANDIES:
  Buttermilk Fudge, 37
  Chocolate-Covered Espresso Beans, 41
  Christmas Tree Suckers, 72
  Monogrammed Toffee, 21
  Peppermint Fudge, 58
  Popcorn Icicles, 89
  Popcorn Wreaths, 71
  "Stained Glass" Brittle, 17
  "Stained Glass" Wreaths, 93
  White Chocolate Popcorn Balls, 19
Cheddar Spread, 33
Cheery Cherry Jam, 38
Cherry Cardinal Cakes, 83
Chocolate-Almond Coffee Mix, 25
Chocolate-Covered Espresso Beans, 41
Chocolate Eggnog, 66
Chocolate-Mint Cheese Ball Mix, 18
Chocolate Snowball Cookies, 65
Christmas Punch, 78
Christmas Tree Suckers, 72
CONDIMENTS:
  Cheery Cherry Jam, 38
  Cranberry Chutney, 12
  Cranberry Vinaigrette, 26
  Strawberry Spread, 43
COOKIES:
  Apple-Cinnamon Cookies, 11
  Chocolate Snowball Cookies, 65
  Gingerbread Cookies, 70
  Gingerbread Nativity, 91
  Orange-Gingerbread Gnomes, 89
  Potato Chip Cookies, 32
  Teapot Cookies, 56
Cranberry-Champagne Cocktails, 66
Cranberry Chutney, 12
Cranberry Vinaigrette, 26

D

Deep-Dish Vegetable Pie, 50
**DESSERTS AND DESSERT TOPPINGS (Se
also Cakes, Candies, Cookies, Pies):**
  Brandied Strawberries, 8
  Orange Black Bottom Pie, 67
  Peaches and Cream Soufflés, 57
  Pear-Ginger Pie, 74
  Peppermint Stick Sauce, 23
  Pumpkin Cheesecake Squares, 61
Doggie Biscuits, 13

E-F

ENTRÉES:
  Deep-Dish Vegetable Pie, 50
  Roasted Cornish Hens with Coriander
    Glaze, 79
  Southwestern Chicken Casserole, 75
  Spinach-Artichoke Casserole, 60
FUDGE:
  Buttermilk Fudge, 37
  Peppermint Fudge, 58

G-I

Gingerbread Cookies, 70
Gingerbread Nativity, 91
Glazed Lemon Cheesecake, 52
Grasshopper Pie, 64
Honey-of-a-Punch, 49
Italian Cheese Snacks, 39

CREDITS

We want to extend a warm thank you to the generous people who allowed us to photograph our projects at their homes: Carl and Monte Brunck, John and Anne Childs, Joan Gould, Paul and Becky Owen, and Dr. Reed and Becky Thompson.

A word of thanks goes to Fifth Season of Little Rock, Arkansas, for the use of the dishes shown in *An Evening of Song*.

To Magna IV Engravers of Little Rock, Arkansas, we say thank you for the superb color reproduction and excellent pre-press preparation.

We want to especially thank photographers Ken West, Larry Pennington, Mark Mathews, and Karen Busick Shirey of Peerless Photography, Little Rock, Arkansas, for their time, patience, and excellent work.

To the talented people who helped in the creation of the following recipes and projects in this book, we extend a special word of thanks.

Snowman Bread, page 22: Glenda Warren
Silver Bells Punch, page 57: Patti Sowers
Gingerbread Cookies, page 70: Lois Sager
Strawberry Punch, page 71: Dorothy Toll

Christmas Tree Mug, page 25, and *Joyous Noel Ornament*, page 43: Polly Carbonari
Fruity Coasters, page 35: Kathy Rose Bradley

We extend a sincere thank you to the people who assisted in making and testing the projects in this book: Jennie Black, Mary Carlton, Kelly Hepner, Kathy Jones, Tera Dawn Phillips, Cathy Smith, and Debra Smith.